IN MY OPINION

IN MY OPINION

An Inquiry into the Contemporary Novel

BY

Orville Prescott

Essay Index Reprint Series

BOOKS FOR LIBRARIES PRESS
FREEPORT, NEW YORK

INTERNATIONAL STANDARD BOOK NUMBER:
0-8369-2014-7

LIBRARY OF CONGRESS CATALOG CARD NUMBER:
73-111857

PRINTED IN THE UNITED STATES OF AMERICA

To

MY MOTHER

Who has always thought that it was a good idea for me to write about books and who, as a mother should, usually likes what I write about them.

ACKNOWLEDGMENTS

I wish to thank the *New York Times* for permission to include material which originally appeared in the "Books of the Times" column, much of it in somewhat different form.

I thank The Macmillan Company, New York, for permission to quote "In Time of 'The Breaking of Nations'" from *Collected Poems of Thomas Hardy;* Harcourt, Brace and Company, Inc., for permission to quote from *1984* by George Orwell and from *The Just and the Unjust* and *Guard of Honor* by James Gould Cozzens; William Sloane Associates, Inc., for permission to quote from *The Big Sky* by A. B. Guthrie, Jr.; and E. P. Dutton and Company for permission to quote from a ballad by Bryan MacMahon, author of *The Lion Tamer.*

I also wish to thank my wife. No writer's wife, I feel sure, ever bore with better grace her husband's continual preoccupation with his task. Without the sound critical insight with which she read these pages as they were written they would now be disfigured by many more shortcomings than they are.

CONTENTS

IN MY OPINION

INTRODUCTION

This is a work of limited scope in which I have made no effort to be comprehensive about so large a subject as the contemporary novel. Nevertheless, the title is accurate. The following pages are about contemporary novels. But they also are about certain aspects of modern thought which I believe the novels reflect. These are the influential and intellectually fashionable ideas which make up that complex and abstract whole which is often called "the modern mind."

But, since it is impossible for any individual, even a reasonably industrious literary critic, to read all the important and significant books of his time, practical limitations have to be acknowledged. Most of the books and authors discussed in the following pages are English, Irish and American, because most of the books I read and find interesting are English, Irish and American. Nearly all of them were published between 1940 and 1951. And most of the books are novels.

Some people hold the dreary and erroneous opinion that fiction is a light and inferior variety of reading, that it is more educational and even more virtuous to read a topical book of current reporting (perhaps already out of date) than to read even the finest novel. It is true that books which report the agonized spasms of our troubled world and books which diagnose its ailments and prescribe treatments are often important and interesting. But they also are often ephemeral, mistaken and downright pigheaded. They have nothing to do with the art of literature.

And today fiction is the most important, popular, influential and characteristic form of literary expression. Few first-rate talents are represented on the modern stage. Modern poets seem to have withdrawn from the world into private arcana of their own where they squat in circles, polishing their symbols and puzzling out one another's cryptograms. The novelists remain in nearly undisputed possession of the literary stage.

It seems to me almost axiomatic that the ablest creative writers today are nearly all novelists. And novelists are more sensitive than the rest of us to the winds of doctrine and the intellectual and moral climate of our time. They are more acute observers of the life around them than ordinary men. Their books are guideposts to their times. And because novelists are widely read they help to shape contemporary culture. It would be a brave and ignorant man who claimed that Dickens did not help to mold the Victorian world, that Sinclair Lewis did not influence the thinking of his countrymen during the 1920s. Even bad novels with extremely serious things wrong with them can be interesting and important.

Radio, television and the movies may have depressingly large audiences. They may be potentially the most important of all art forms, because of their power for good or evil. But right now, halfway through the twentieth century, fiction remains the queen of the creative arts.

So in the following pages some novelists are discussed who seem to me significant for their artistic achievement, their influence and the ideas which they champion. Some of the verdicts rendered here are unfavorable, for I believe that some of our most talented writers are artistically befuddled and intellectually confused.

If literary criticism were only the noble pleasure of praising,

Introduction

as Swinburne once incautiously said it was, the feuds and tribal wars which are a permanent feature of the world of books would expire from lack of nourishment. Luckily, there is no danger of such an insipid state of affairs ever afflicting us; for criticism deals with combustible matters, emotion and opinion. Aspire to judicious objectivity as he may, the critic cannot help reacting emotionally to literary stimuli; he cannot help expressing opinions which are personal to him and so anathema to others.

"Love me, love my dog" cuts close to something basic in human nature. In the world of books it can be rendered: find faults in my pet author and I will doubt your sanity and hate your viscera. From Aristotle and Longinus to the youngest critic bristling with righteous indignation there has never been a standard critical foot rule by which writing can be judged. Wide acquaintance with books, enthusiasm for them and honesty in judging them are about the only qualifications most critics have in common.

So this is a personal and opinionated book. I don't expect anyone to agree with all of it. I won't be surprised if some disagree with most of it.

After all, Jonathan Swift, as he did on so many subjects, wrote some true words about literary criticism: "That was excellently observed, say I, when I read a passage in an author, where his opinion agrees with mine. When we differ, there I pronounce him to be mistaken."

I

THE NOVELIST'S WORLD

"In Time of 'The Breaking of Nations'"

There is no such thing, of course, as "the modern mind." There are many minds and some of them seem almost prehistoric. People think differently in different countries and in different parts of the same country. Their occupations, their education, their religious convictions and their degree of awareness of current ideas and current problems vary enormously. A credulous reader of the *Chicago Tribune* would not often agree with a credulous reader of the New York *Daily Worker*. The great abstraction which we call the modern mind is divided into many parts.

Those whose thinking is part of the modern mind are those who read and write and think, who question and worry, and who, because they are articulate, influence one another and the culture of their time. Teachers and clergymen, novelists and journalists, scientists and social workers, doctors and lawyers, corporation presidents and labor leaders—all are influenced by the factors which make ours an "age of anxiety."

Whole libraries of books have been written analyzing the crisis of modern civilization. Such an analysis has no place here, even if I were qualified to make it. It must be enough to point out once more that we are the victims of world-shattering catastrophes and the inheritors of a series of fantastically explosive ideas.

We have witnessed two cruelly destructive world wars, the collapse of ancient empires and the rise of a moloch state which threatens to enslave us all. We have seen the havoc of the world's worst depression and the confusion of new experiments in economics and politics. We have witnessed the monstrously efficient barbarism of fascism and communism. We have stared in fear and awe at the portentous spectacle of demonic powers unleashed by learned physicists who seem to feel more guilt than pride in their achievement. The winds of wrath are blowing shrilly through the ruins of the world and the history of contemporary man is reckoned in a series of shattering explosions. The illusion of economic security was swept away in the high wind of 1929. And now even the hope of physical security is feeble indeed. To survive is beginning to seem no mean achievement. These are the events which have rent the fabric of modern civilization. Some of them had their origin in the ideas of a few momentously influential men.

Sometimes it seems that the two men whose ideas and examples have most influenced twentieth-century thought were Machiavelli and Genghis Khan. But so erroneous and cynical a notion comes only at black moments induced by a careful reading of the morning newspaper. We know that the intellectual, moral and spiritual world in which we live has been profoundly shaped by the thought of a few men considerably more influential.

From Copernicus and Luther down through the centuries a series of great men has been busily at work changing the world: changing man's conception of his place in it, whittling away at his ego, at his sense of personal responsibility and at the foundations of his most cherished beliefs. They have abolished the small, safe and tidy world of the past, with its established rules and numerous comforting certainties, and put chaos in its place.

Most of us would agree, I think, that four men outrank all others as leaders of our interlocked intellectual revolutions. They are: Darwin, whose theory of evolution is the keystone in the arch of scientific materialism, who did more than any other man to weaken faith in revealed religion; Marx, whose theory of inevitable proletarian revolution changed the economic and social thinking of the world and provided a sacred scripture for the no longer very Marxian religion preached from Moscow; Freud, whose theories about the unconscious mind, the significance of sex, of dreams, and the importance of infantile and childhood experience created a new psychology of man which infiltrated the entire Western world until even schoolboys talked of their complexes; and Einstein, who was understood by so few and misunderstood by so many, but who seemed to most people to be saying that the certainties of science as they had been accepted were no longer certain—even that the physical universe was infinitely mysterious and "relative."

Largely because of the momentum of Darwin's and Marx's ideas, many modern men came to believe in the littleness and helplessness of man, an unimportant animal subject to laws of heredity and environment which ruled his life completely. Largely because of Freud many modern men came to believe that character is largely accidental, that instinctive drives are supreme, that codes of honor are only social conventions and that moral obligations are only words. Largely because of Einstein many modern men came to believe that the universe is an appalling and incomprehensible mystery. And a host of

[18]

astronomers, anthropologists, psychologists, psychoanalysts, economists and sociologists have ventured farther down the trails blazed by the four great pioneers.

They drove back the boundaries of ignorance and immeasurably widened man's intellectual horizons. Most of what they discovered is probably true; some of it is probably mistaken and will be disproved by future discoveries. It has been exciting and stimulating to live in an epoch as intellectually revolutionary as ours. But it has not been comfortable.

In fact, it has been so uncomfortable that many modern men seem to be suffering from a crisis neurosis. They are frightened by their unbelief. They do not believe in organized religion, in the beneficent powers of science, in the idea of inevitable progress, in the strength and virtue of a democratic, capitalistic society, in the traditional forms of art and even in traditional standards of morality. Lost in a wilderness of doubt and relativity, they cringe and cower before the dreadful spectacle of their own pessimism and despair.

Such behavior, it seems to me, is obviously decadent. When a considerable percentage of the best informed and most highly educated members of a society have no faith in the values on which their society was built, none in its strength or health and none in themselves, it is futile to deny that decadence is present. Decadence is not just a matter of sexual abnormality; although sometimes openly flaunted sexual abnormality is one manifestation of decadence. It is a matter of lost confidence and lost energy.

So far our modern decadence has infected only part of our civilization. Many people still face life and its horrible possibilities with courage and optimism. A fighting faith in the values of our free society and in the dignity and worth of individual men and women may yet sweep in a reinvigorating flame across the world. And if such collective salvation ever comes it must bring with it a restored emphasis on moral values.

Philosophers, psychologists and anthropologists endlessly debate the origin of moral standards and often find them only in social pressures and tribal taboos. But simple and wise men both have always known that love and loyalty, kindness and brotherhood, honesty and generosity are good; that hatred, cruelty, selfishness and treachery are evil. Even if we do not know what are the ultimate sanctions of ethical conduct, it should be obvious that a sense of moral obligation based upon these convictions is essential. The decay of such a moral sense is one of the fundamental causes of our present plight. When standards of ethical conduct lose their social force, when ideas of what is right and wrong become mired in a morass of relativism, determinism and environment, then civilization is endangered, then might impersonates right again and the dogs of war are more frequently let loose.

These, then, are the most important elements which combine to make "the modern mind." Novelists are even more troubled and confused by them than the rest of us. Often they are serious students of some particular aspect of modern thought, many reading deeply in Freud. Others make a conscientious study of politics and foreign affairs and reflect their conclusions in their books. In the following pages we will discuss the various ways in which a number of modern novelists have tried to solve the perplexing problem of how to write fiction in times which try men's souls. A work of fiction is a story about human beings. And human beings, no matter how dark the skies above them, no matter how fearful the carnage in the next field, never cease attending to the ordinary tasks of daily living. Perhaps it would be a useful reminder of this for readers and writers alike if they turned back occasionally and reread Thomas Hardy's poem "In Time of 'The Breaking of Nations' ":

> "Only a man harrowing clods
>   In a slow silent walk
> With an old horse that stumbles and nods
>   Half asleep as they stalk.
>
> Only thin smoke without flame
>   From the heaps of couch-grass;
> Yet this will go onward the same
>   Though Dynasties pass.
>
> Yonder a maid and her wight
>   Come whispering by:
> War's annals will fade into night
>   Ere their story die."

II

THE POLITICAL NOVEL:

Warren, Orwell, Koestler

"The blood of citizens is the mortar wherewith the governments of tyrants is cemented. Let every man therefore do what he can that no edifice of this sort be built in his city."—*Francisco Guicciardini,* 1492-1540

Twenty years ago the depression taught many of us that economics is not just the dismal science, that it is bread. Since then fascism and communism have been teaching us that politics is not just a sordid game played on a national stage, that it is life itself. Novelists learned these lessons so well that the political novel has become more important in our time than it has ever been before.

The political novel is nothing new under the sun. Balzac and Trollope wrote of politics and many a Utopian idealist has presented his dreams in the guise of fiction. But the portentous importance of modern politics has given novels which deal with it an urgency which their predecessors lacked.

There are two principal varieties of political fiction: novels about characters involved in politics and so about politics themselves; and novels designed to persuade their readers to share their authors' political convictions, novels which are primarily propaganda pamphlets. Examples of the first are the works of Robert Penn Warren. The second far larger category is best represented by the novels of George Orwell and Arthur Koestler.

There has been more sheer unmitigated nonsense written about political fiction in the last twenty years than about any other kind. Most of it was based on the elementary error of refusing to recognize that political fiction must be judged upon two entirely separate counts: its merits as a contribution to political thought, if any, and its merits as a work of fiction. All too often we have seen critics make fools of themselves by praising novels because they approved their political message, when the novels themselves were so ludicrously bad that any angry high-school student with a typewriter could have written them. The worst critical aberrations of this nature took place in the 1930s when the so-called proletarian novels, which were never written by proletarians, were praised by proletarian critics, who weren't proletarian either. Writers with soft hearts and thick heads had succumbed to the fraudulent blandishments of communism and actually believed that communism offered a high-minded solution to the problems of the depression. Naturally, then, any novel about a hungry laborer and a wicked capitalist was a masterpiece.

When the depression retreated before the gigantic government spending caused by war, the proletarian novel disappeared. There were so few good ones, anyway, that only John Steinbeck's and John Dos Passos' are now remembered. In their place came antifascist novels and, as the true nature of communism became more generally understood, anticommunist novels. By a fortunate chance the sounder politics of these was matched by the much greater literary ability of their authors.

But even the best political novels devoted to the good fight against fascism and communism have not been notable as works of literary art.

The reason for this, it seems to me, is a matter of motive and inspiration. The really basic literary drive is interest in the eternally fascinating problem of human personality, in creating characters and telling stories about them. When a novelist conceives of his characters first, becomes absorbed in them and then proceeds to write about their lives in a particular set of circumstances he may produce a fine novel. And he may shed interesting and significant light on his characters' environment, cultural, economic or political, in the process.

But when a novelist plans to denounce an evil or plead for a cause and then hunts around for characters who will demonstrate his message he rarely makes his characters believable or interesting. They usually remain stiff puppets acting out his political parable, dull and unreal. The creative magic of successful fiction has failed to take place. The politics has driven out the art. But sometimes a novelist can be such an able political journalist and can write with such fierce passion about politics that his books are powerful and important, in spite of the fact that they are clumsy and unsuccessful as works of art. Harriet Beecher Stowe demonstrated this in *Uncle Tom's Cabin* a hundred years ago. George Orwell and Arthur Koestler have done the same in recent years.

Robert Penn Warren, Kentucky-born and Tennessee-educated, is a poet, a critic and a professor of English as well as a novelist. Like so many Southern writers, he is obsessed by the shortcomings of the South; but he writes about them with an eloquence and an elemental rage worlds apart from the sordid bitterness of some of his literary colleagues. The subject matter of his principal books is the moral significance of particular political and social behavior.

And to their composition he has applied uncommon talents: a headlong narrative pace which makes his novels intensely readable, a fierce emotion which charges his pages with contagious tension and an exuberant delight in poetic imagery. Until the present none of Mr. Warren's novels has been entirely successful. But all of them convey the impression of a richly gifted writer considering an important theme, of having been "written." Too many modern novels seem to have been thrown together in sloppy haste or ground out of a sausage machine by someone nearly too tired to turn the crank.

The faults of Mr. Warren's novels seem complementary to their virtues. Often one feels that their author has become so fascinated with verbal effects that he overdoes them; that he is so interested in some of his characters, often minor ones, that he neglects to make the others as convincingly motivated and persuasive as they should be; that he spends too much time in irrelevant digressions. And in his best and most important novel, *All the King's Men,* there is a disturbing refusal to face the most important political significance of the central character.

In *At Heaven's Gate* Mr. Warren wrote a terrible and engrossing story of moral decadence, business fraud and social degeneration, which somehow lost effectiveness because it seemed grossly exaggerated. Instead of the angry and pointed exposure of a decadent society which Mr. Warren must have intended it to be, *At Heaven's Gate* is only a thumping melodrama, entertaining, but hardly to be taken seriously.

All the King's Men is much more impressive. This is a novel about the cracker dictator of a Southern state, its hero obviously and closely modeled on Huey Long. The Willie Stark of Mr.

[25]

Warren's story is a magnificently rendered character, vital, swaggering, sometimes idealistic, and always ruthlessly corrupt. His dramatic story and the part he played in the lives of numerous people and in the life of his state are all extremely well told. Mr. Warren's ear for spoken English is superb and so are some of his own rhetorical flights. But three key characters, all of them aristocrats trampled down by Willie in his rush to power, are stiff and wooden and unbelievable. The continuously astonishing thing about Mr. Warren's writing is that it can be so uneven. Some of it is so good; some of it is so flat.

The political significance of *All the King's Men* depends on Mr. Warren's interpretation of Willie. He has conveyed well Willie's great abilities and primitive idealism, combined with his bottomless greed and lust for power. He has not overlooked Willie's moral degradation of his state, his use of bribery, blackmail and force, his contemptuous destruction of freedom and decency. But Mr. Warren magnifies the roads, schools, income taxes, etc., introduced in Willie's regime. "At least the Boss does something," says one of Mr. Warren's characters. He might have said, "The trains run on time." Mr. Warren has missed completely the most significant thing about Willie Stark and Huey Long, their personification of the American road toward fascism.

If *All the King's Men* is less than it might have been, it is at least arresting and provocative. As much cannot be said for its successor, *World Enough and Time*. This, too, is a novel about politics, and even more flamboyantly melodramatic. It is the story of a sensational murder trial in Kentucky in the 1820s based on an actual and celebrated case. Its young hero is involved in a whole series of moral issues, problems of ends and means, truth and honor, private or public justice. But his brooding on these matters is muddled, inconclusive and dull. And the excitement of his violent adventures is much diminished by two damaging literary shortcomings. Both hero and heroine of this romantic melodrama are stiff and inhuman. They stalk through this violent story like ghosts without arousing sympathy or interest. It is the minor characters who are lusty, amusing and real.

The other reason why *World Enough and Time* is sadly disappointing is its florid style. In many quotations from imaginary documents Mr. Warren brilliantly parodies the romantic rhetoric of the period. But he fails to guard against its contagion. Much of his own narrative is lushly overwritten. Robert Penn Warren has not yet written the fine and fully integrated novel of which he seems capable.

Nor did George Orwell ever write an artistically successful novel, but he was a provocative writer. A stimulating, dogmatic and stubbornly Marxist literary critic and essayist, a powerful political propagandist and an indifferent novelist, Orwell could not be fitted into any literary pigeonhole. He was modest to eccentricity. Orwell was a pseudonym. His real name was Eric Blair. In the British *Who's Who* he withheld the customary data about the date of his birth, his parentage, his career and address. But it is known that he studied at Eton, that he served in the British Civil Service in Burma and despised what he saw of British rule there, that he knew desperate poverty in Paris and London, that he was a doctrinaire Marxist ("Private property is an obstructive nuisance"). Yet, in spite of his Marxism, Orwell was a bitter foe of every variety of totalitarianism.

Orwell's political and literary ideas may be found in two collections of critical essays, *Dickens, Dali, and Others* and

Shooting an Elephant and Other Essays. These volumes contain about as many prejudices as they do ideas. Orwell was tough, disillusioned and cynical. He believed in little except mankind and the need for socialism. Although he hated and understood totalitarianism, Orwell always clung to the belief that socialism and democracy were compatible. His background of poverty and Marxism prevented him from recognizing that complete socialism would entrust such fantastic power to the state that only politicians of saintly character could keep it from degenerating into a totalitarian tyranny. It was a blind spot in the vision of a man who loathed politics and politicians, and who believed that "politics itself is a mass of lies, evasions, folly, hatred and schizophrenia."

Nevertheless, in spite of their prejudices and dubious generalizations, Orwell's essays are frequently brilliant, trenchant, original in point of view and intellectually stimulating. Orwell was not always right, but he always wrote well. His angry, piercing voice will be missed for a long time. And one book he wrote will be long remembered, the novel called *1984.*

It was actually his second fictional attack on the totalitarian state. The first was an elementary little parable which satirized Soviet political history in terms of a fairy tale about a revolution of farmyard animals in which two pigs played the roles of Trotsky and Stalin. On the whole, *Animal Farm* is a mildly amusing and quite superficial performance. Orwell did not seem clear in his own mind why the revolution ended in tyranny. The totalitarian regime of the pigs could have come about either through the wickedness of the pigs and the stupidity of the other animals, or through the very nature of a revolution by force instead of through peaceable evolution. But when Orwell wrote *1984* he did not have to concern himself with the origin

[28]

of a totalitarian state. His interest was in making clear the true character of totalitarianism and the ultimate horror inherent in its antihuman philosophy.

1984 is a fantasy about the future. It includes numerous examples of future scientific developments and so it could be placed with some justice in that popular bargain basement of literature called science fiction. But Orwell's future is not the kind Utopian authors used to portray when they contrasted the unhappy present with the bliss to come. Not so long ago Utopia was just around the corner; if science could not solve our problems, political and social reorganization could. But that was in another century, and now such hopes are dead. Today our dismal present seems as alluring as the Moslem paradise compared with our fears of what the future may bring. And the two things which frighten us most about the future are the two which so recently inspired hope—science and political and economic reorganization.

In *1984* Orwell did not write a subtle or finished novel about human beings. Its characters are wooden and its joints creak. But as a political analysis, a prophecy and a warning it is superb. It portrays the ultimate degradation of a totalitarian state with repulsive power.

It isn't just a question of horrors. There would be little profit in still another description of secret police, concentration camps and death factories. What Orwell did was to extend into the future with remorseless clarity of vision trends which are already apparent in the present. Most of those trends he found in Nazi Germany and Communist Russia, a few of them, perhaps, almost without his realizing it, in British socialism. He showed how the collective state run by a ruling class of managers soon forgets the good of the people and concentrates on power for the rulers. He showed how much farther the cult of power for its own sake can go than even contemporaries of Hitler imagine. He showed how individuals can be broken, corrupted and even converted by torture, not just tormented and killed.

It is this vivid, sickening, chilling exploration of absolute depravity which gives *1984* its gruesome fascination. The depravity of the rulers of Orwell's future state was only in part a matter of sadism. It lay primarily in their contempt for human beings, their delight in destroying their victims' minds and characters, not just in enslaving them. As one of "The Inner Party," a master of psychological as well of physical torture, said:

"Power is not a means; it is an end. One does not establish a dictatorship in order to safeguard a revolution; one makes the revolution to establish the dictatorship. The object of persecution is persecution. The object of power is power. . . . How does one man assert his power over another? . . . By making him suffer. Obedience is not enough. Unless he is suffering, how can you be sure that he is obeying your will and not his own? Power is in inflicting pain and humiliation. . . . All competing pleasure will be destroyed. But always—do not forget this, Winston—always there will be the intoxication of power, constantly increasing and constantly growing subtler. Always, at every moment, there will be the thrill of victory, the sensation of trampling on an enemy who is helpless. If you want a picture of the future, imagine a boot stamping on a human face—forever."

The reason this passage is so awful is that it does not seem like grotesque exaggeration. It may be madness; but it is convincing madness. Knowing what has happened already in this century, one believes in Orwell's madman. One believes and finds the pitiless last section of *1984* unspeakably dreadful. *1984* is not a landmark in creative fiction; it is one of the most powerful political pamphlets ever written.

Just as *1984* is the most effective antitotalitarian novel of our time so *Darkness at Noon* is the finest novel yet written about the psychology of the totalitarian mind. It is also the finest novel yet written by Arthur Koestler, who is certainly the ablest and much the most influential of all modern writers who use fiction for political purposes.

Arthur Koestler was born in Hungary in 1905. He is a graduate of the University of Vienna, and also of the strife and misery and intellectual and moral confusion which have swept like a pestilence across Central Europe for thirty-five years. A journalist, an intellectual and a leftist, Mr. Koestler looked around him in his youth at the ruins of collapsed societies and the disintegration of social classes and succumbed with passionate gullibility to an infection in the very air. If Utopia existed in Russia and the Nazis were about to make an inferno of Germany he wanted to fight on the side of the angels. While he worked as a newspaper reporter in the 1930s he was an enrolled member of the Communist Party for six years and did not lose his last illusion until after the Russian-German pact of 1939. He knew at first hand all there was to be known about the conspiratorial methods and intellectual bondage of the Party. Mr. Koestler may have learned the importance of freedom and the monstrous significance of communism slowly; but he learned well. Today he is one of the most effective foes of communism in the world. "We ex-Communists," he says with some truth, "are the only people on your side who know what it is all about."

To have been a Communist and no longer to be one seems to

be one of the most intense and painful of psychological experiences. It means that the ex-Communist has submitted to a discipline which controlled his thoughts as well as his actions, which demanded arduous self-sacrifice; and it means that he has made a protestation of faith as complete as that of a Catholic priest. For a Party member to revolt against Communist discipline and to renounce the Communist faith is frequently as soul-shattering as comparable behavior would be for a member of the Society of Jesus. Former Communists are not as other men are. They bear a burden of guilt which they can never shake off. They have sinned and their sin is heresy.

Consequently among all the rootless drifters tossed about by the turmoil of our time the most emotionally bitter and the most intellectually lonely are the disillusioned Communists. Once they thought that they were marching in a great crusade, and then they discovered that they had been the dupes of unscrupulous hypocrites who hid their voracious lust for power behind a mask of reforming zeal. Many of the former Communists still cling to their belief in some exalted form of socialism, although they renounce the form which socialism took in Russia.

The original conversion of many of them had been based on ignorance, on a generous desire to help cure the evils of the world and on an emotional longing for political salvation. This longing often seems to have had an element of hysteria about it, an irrational craving for dogmatic answers to all doubts, for authority, for an escape from personal responsibility. So communism held particular attractions for the emotionally unstable, the credulous and ignorant and the youthfully idealistic. Among these last the most intelligent have found out for themselves the true nature of communism and the most courageous among the intelligent have repudiated it.

The Political Novel

When Arthur Koestler writes novels he never does so with the purely artistic, character-creating motives generally identified with fictional inspiration. For him a novel is a soapbox or a pulpit from which he can preach about the issues of our time. To clarify by dramatizing, to denounce by exposing, to interpret by analyzing seem to be Mr. Koestler's basic intentions. And so, like nearly all novelists who are primarily propagandists, Mr. Koestler has not been very successful in creating individual characters. He has been so intent on seeing that his characters represent particular points of view that he has failed to make them interesting as particular human beings. But Mr. Koestler is so powerful a writer, so fiercely honest a thinker and so eloquent a crusader that his novels are always stirring and provocative in spite of their limitations. They may not be memorable as works of art, but the fiery blast of their emotion and the brutally shocking clarity of their reporting make them important documents on our unhappy age, significant interpretations of the world's agony.

Arthur Koestler's first book, *The Gladiators,* went almost unnoticed when it was first published in 1939. It was an historical novel about Spartacus and the revolt of the slaves and gladiators in the first century b.c. Although it was an artfully indirect apology for communism written while Mr. Koestler still clung to his faith, *The Gladiators* displayed much of the emotional urgency and intellectual power which have marked all his subsequent works. His second novel was *Darkness at Noon,* which was published in 1941.

Few novels have had more vital significance for their authors than *Darkness at Noon.* It marked Mr. Koestler's public repudiation of the Party. And few works of fiction have had such political significance for the world at large. *Darkness at Noon*

[33]

offered the most convincing explanation which has yet been made of the extraordinary "confessions" made by the old Bolsheviks in the famous Moscow purge trials of the 1930s.

Darkness at Noon is the story of the last days in a Moscow prison of Rubashov, an old Bolshevik, a hero of the civil war and one of the Party's principal leaders since long before the revolution. It is told entirely from Rubashov's point of view, partly through his memories of the past, mostly concentrated on each step by which Rubashov is persuaded to confess falsely that he is a traitor who has participated in an organized conspiracy to assassinate Stalin.

As a dramatic narrative *Darkness at Noon* is short, tense and so expertly constructed that it drives remorselessly toward its pitiful denouement. Its characterization of Rubashov is superb, Mr. Koestler's best and only completely successful creation of an unforgettable individual. And as a demonstration of the moral surrender and intellectual corruption which communism inflicts upon its true believers it is appalling.

Rubashov was brave and intelligent, but a fanatic who had never hesitated to kill and betray in the service of his cause. He had always believed that the end justifies the means, that individuals do not matter, that "the Party can never be mistaken." But he had thought that Stalin's dictatorship was a technical deviation from the proper goals of the Party. *Darkness at Noon* shows in a series of interviews between Rubashov and his official inquisitor how Rubashov was brought step by step to the conviction that he might be mistaken, that Stalin's regime *was* the continuing Party and that it was his duty to the Party, the last service which he owed it, to lie and disgrace himself in a final gesture of self-sacrifice. Psychologically gruesome and sickening though it is, *Darkness at Noon* is also psychologically persuasive. This, one is convinced, is the way it must have been.

Arthur Koestler's next two books were both autobiographical accounts of personal experiences with the new barbarism which has infected modern European politics. In *Dialogue with Death* he described his harrowing experiences in Franco's Spain during the Spanish civil war when he was confined in two different prisons under sentence of death. And in *Scum of the Earth* he wrote of his sufferings in a French concentration camp during the early days of the "phony war" in 1940. As an alien, as a fugitive from Hitler and an outspoken antifascist, and as a leftist of only very recent anticommunist convictions, Mr. Koestler seemed ideal concentration-camp material to the French bureaucrats, who did not realize how much more deeply committed he was to fighting France's enemies than were most Frenchmen.

The third Koestler novel, *Arrival and Departure,* is a direct reflection of its author's search for a new faith. For the slavish worship of the gods of the Kremlin he substituted a crusade against both brown and red totalitarianism. And being mentally and spiritually tormented by his recent apostasy he sought guidance and understanding in Freudian psychology. *Arrival and Departure* is theoretically a study in the sources of courage; actually it is another milestone in the pilgrimage of Arthur Koestler through the valley of giants and the slough of despair.

As a work of literature *Arrival and Departure* is stiff, artificial and intermittently tedious. Although its accounts of torture and massacre are among the most terrible ever written, its central situation seems wonderfully unreal and arbitrarily contrived. What, asks Mr. Koestler, enables his hero, whose courage is a legend in the underground, to bear the utmost agony of Gestapo torture? A handy psychiatrist explains, too patly, that the hero's courage is inspired by an inner need to atone for a sense of guilt dating from childhood. Once this is understood, the hero's compulsion to sacrifice himself in the good fight against tyranny is ended. He can flee to America. But he does not, he returns to the underground nobly determined to help purge the world of its abominations. The courage of blindness has been replaced by the courage of altruistic vision. Mr. Koestler's hero has repeated his creator's own life pattern. *Arrival and Departure* is one of Mr. Koestler's most deeply felt political parables; but it is the most inept and clumsy of his novels.

In a collection of political and literary essays called *The Yogi and the Commissar* Mr. Koestler abjured and denounced the end-justifies-the-means philosophy of the world's commissars, the equivocal double talk by which they justify their use of force and fraud. And he also rejected the other extreme, the yogi's withdrawal from the heat and dust of the fray into mystic concentration on spiritual concepts. A middle way must be found, Mr. Koestler insisted. The best he could find was "a true socialist movement."

This limp and conventionally idealistic conclusion was hardly an astute or constructive contribution to political thought. Whatever "true socialism" may be, it is not an oriflamme around which all men of good will can rally. Too many would be arguing about what it is, and too many others would be sulking in their tents, reluctant to fight until and unless they approved the future division of the spoils. Mr. Koestler is at his best only on the offensive, exposing the horrors of fascism and communism. Usually, but not always, he is too emotionally involved for objective political thought. And who isn't these days?

[36]

How strongly his emotions can color his thought Mr. Koestler showed in his next novel, *Thieves in the Night*. As a report on the Zionist communes of Palestine during the Arab warfare of the late 1930s *Thieves in the Night* is able. It dramatizes well the fanatical zeal and self-sacrifice which lay behind the Jews' remarkable achievements in Palestine. But it is a mediocre novel. Its fictional method is only a transparent disguise for its political reporting. And its political significance is highly questionable.

This is the story of Joseph, an intellectual cobbler whose fanatical fury increased until he enlisted in the Stern Group of terrorists. Mr. Koestler might say that he was only trying to show how suffering, loyalty, hatred and desire for revenge drove Joseph to act as he did. But the entire tenor of *Thieves in the Night* is one of sympathetic admiration for its hero. Joseph argues that terror is necessary in our present ice age, that bloody nationalism will be of lasting benefit to the Jews—which are fascist arguments. Joseph justified the despicable methods of terrorism by the hypothetically worthy end he hoped to gain. He had unwittingly joined the commissars. And Mr. Koestler, by not making it clear that he deplored Joseph's conduct, seemed to do so, too. The special case of Palestine, where his sympathies were intensely involved, had confused his moral vision, or it at least confused his presentation of the issue in *Thieves in the Night*.

Much more objective and better balanced was Mr. Koestler's history of the Zionist movement and the state of Israel, *Promise and Fulfilment*. This lively journalistic work was as clear and judicious as *Thieves in the Night* was not. This time Mr. Koestler was just, if hardly merciful, to the Arabs and the British. And much frank criticism seasoned his sympathetic account of

[37]

the Zionists. And, as if he remembered his earlier mistake, Mr. Koestler was particularly careful not to condone terrorism while at the same time he explained its origin and background.

Of his gigantic *Insight and Outlook* little need be said. It was an amazingly learned, though amateur, attempt to make a contribution to philosophy and psychology. Heavily loaded with technical jargon and sententious obscurities, it sank of its own weight. Even Koestler enthusiasts could not face so formidably dense a book.

Early in 1951 still another work was added to the astonishing output of this indefatigable writer. *The Age of Longing* is a novel of the near future, of "the middle nineteen-fifties." A bitter prophecy of doom and a melancholy lament for the lost hopes of European civilization, it is a study of fear and degeneration and moral paralysis. It does not manifest the shrill and hysterical despair which has infected a number of lesser European writers. Its despair is of another kind, a sort of cold and stoic resignation to the inevitable. Like the Spartans at Thermopylae, Mr. Koestler seems to be fighting grimly from a sense of duty with no expectation of much good coming from his efforts.

The Age of Longing is gruesomely interesting, intellectually disturbing, spattered with brilliant bits. But, like all Mr. Koestler's fiction save *Darkness at Noon,* it is crudely uneven and quite mediocre as a creative work of art. In Paris a few years hence the threat of Soviet conquest has become almost unbearable. With morose wit and bludgeoning satire Mr. Koestler pillories the futility of American missions, the agonized waiting for death or slavery of intellectuals and former Communists, the obscene ventriloquism of Communist puppets. And he centers his novel about a problem in faith.

The only hope imaginable to any of his characters is a feeble one: the appearance of a new religion, which would restore to frightened men a reinvigorating faith. Drowning, they clutch at a straw. But the only character in *The Age of Longing* who has the strength, confidence and conviction of perfect faith is a Soviet secret agent completely conditioned to absolute faith in his Party, his state and their ruthless system. Contrasted with this sinister figure, who is both an unscrupulous opportunist and a true believer, is a young American divorcée who has lost her Catholic faith. And midway between these two is a celebrated Russian writer whose wife is a hostage for the conformity of his writings. The writer has no faith and, being older than the secret agent, is less completely conditioned by propaganda and discipline. It is all a neat diagram of Mr. Koestler's thesis.

But it isn't persuasive. Mr. Koestler has drawn a frightening portrait of the agent, a preposterous one of the American girl. Evidently, he knows everything about Communist zealots, hardly anything about American girls. *The Age of Longing* crackles with provocative ideas and chills with the cold blast of its pessimism. Its politics are important and grimly interesting. But it is much too mechanical and stiff to be considered seriously as literary art.

In addition to George Orwell and Arthur Koestler, many others have written political novels in recent years. But since none of them has aroused so much interest or written with such intellectual power it does not seem necessary to discuss them here.

III

THE POWER OF ENVIRONMENT:

Wright, Motley, Wolff, Betty Smith

"As flies to wanton boys, are we to the gods;
They kill us for their sport."—*King Lear*

Novels are never written in a vacuum. They never are
pure art, pure entertainment, completely detached observation.
When a novelist begins typing on page one he is already committed by his own character, his own fiercely cherished convictions, the grand total of his experience of men and books, to a
particular vision of life. His philosophy may be as unformulated
as Jane Austen's, or it may darken his entire horizon as Herman
Melville's did. It may be as superficial as the crude mixture of
socialism and evolution of Jack London, or as profound as the
brooding on character and fate of Joseph Conrad. But, whatever
it may be, some general viewpoint is certain to emerge from
any seriously written novel.

And that is one of the abiding fascinations of fiction. In novels we can escape from a world of irrational confusion into one
of some kind of order and meaning. No matter how different
an author's conception of life may be from our own, we can still
find a sort of artistic satisfaction in the design and purpose he
imposes on his story. Life, in even the blackest and most pessi-

mistic of books, seems to move in some direction and not just to ooze blindly in any, like an amoeba. It seems to be so arranged as to mean something, even if its meaning is only negation and despair. At least as far as the particular book is concerned, the despair itself is meaning. Outside of books few general conclusions are any more certain than that.

Consequently, because his ideas go down so easily, sugar-coated with drama and emotion, the novelist bears a heavy burden of responsibility. He need not conform to any particular, popular credo in politics, economics or religion. But he does have a moral obligation, I believe, to be honest about his writing, to be aware of the implications of his books, and to be certain that he wishes to persuade his readers to accept them. Novelists are powerful teachers. They help to form millions of opinions about man and society. And it is what we think of ourselves that, in the long run, determines the conduct of men and of nations. If we think that individuals are important, that they have faith and loyalty, ideas and ideals and the power of choice, as well as fear, lust and avarice, we can still hope. But if we think of human beings as without responsibility, as entirely subject to forces beyond their control, then they hardly seem worth worrying about.

It is this last idea which is the essence of the literary philosophy called naturalism, the worship of the two-faced god, heredity and environment. A number of extremely able, fiercely honest and profoundly gloomy men have been literary naturalists. Most of them have cared deeply about the unfortunate lot of suffering mankind. They believed that men were nearly powerless to overcome the psychological, social and economic forces which conditioned their lives; but they cared about the miserable creatures anyway. So they wanted to change the

[41]

forces, the environment. Progressive education, slum clearance, collective bargaining and psychoanalysis, these were the world changers summoned at various times to improve the deplorable human environment. And no one would deny that some improvements have been made. And in this the literary naturalists played their part. Their contempt for the intellectual and moral capacity of individual men helped shape the patronizing solicitude for men in the mass, which has been a distinguishing feature of recent history. It is the keystone of the welfare state.

Naturalism is not only a theory about man and society; it is a literary method. Most naturalists from Emile Zola to James T. Farrell have neglected, or have been unable, to create many memorable characters. They have been too intent on producing a sociological report, on itemizing specific facts. Their books are usually long, repetitious and tedious. They lack the selectivity, the compression and implication of true fictional art. They substitute the crude power of documentation for the suggestive power of creative artistry. Their prose is usually flat and pedestrian, graceless, without the rhythms and verbal niceties which mark the work of genuinely distinguished writers. Compared with the beautiful simplicity of Willa Cather's style, for instance, the ponderous prose of Theodore Dreiser is an abomination.

During the last decade the naturalist vogue has shown signs of petering out. James Farrell's most important works, the Studs Lonigan and Danny O'Neill series, were both published in the 1930s. He has written nothing to touch them since. Probably the two most talented naturalist writers of the 1940s were two Negroes, Richard Wright and Willard Motley.

Richard Wright's two principal books are a novel of Negro slum life in Chicago, *Native Son,* and an autobiography, *Black*

[42]

Boy. Both are raw and violent and sickeningly powerful, raging denunciations of the miseries of poverty and the injustices of racial discrimination. Bigger, the "bad Nigger" of *Native Son,* is driven by the desperation, fear and frustration of his unspeakable environment into violent crime. He wasn't a promising character to start with; but Mr. Wright makes it clear that Bigger is a victim of circumstance and therefore not primarily responsible for his character and actions.

But Mr. Wright's autobiography contradicts this argument. *Black Boy* describes a life as miserable and shocking as anything in *Native Son.* Mr. Wright knew every kind of frightful handicap, the sordid barbarities of gruesome poverty, the fear and fawning subservience which are the lot of Negroes in the Deep South. They left him permanently embittered so that his books are filled with grotesque exaggeration and smoldering hatred. But they did not destroy him. Mr. Wright, like most Negroes, did not let his sense of injustice prevent him from becoming a decent citizen. For a short interval he was trapped in the false embrace of communism; but he had the intelligence and courage to repudiate it. And because he was genuinely talented he became a famous writer. The abler naturalist writers are exceptions to their own theories.

Although Willard Motley is a Negro, he has written of a white hero, Nick Romano, in *Knock on Any Door.* Nick was an angel-faced altar boy when he was little. But by the time he was twenty-one he was a gangster and murderer. His descent to perdition roughly parallels Bigger's. And *Knock on Any Door* is an even better novel than *Native Son.* It is raw and brutal and sometimes crude in its denunciation of the sins of society and the perils of an evil environment. But its dramatic

[43]

force, its swaggeringly real characters, and its exciting narrative punch make it memorable. As much cannot be said for Mr. Motley's second novel, *We Fished All Night.*

This incomplete and inchoate book is the raw material for a novel, not a novel itself. Formless, confused, lumpy with undigested facts and ideas, it taxes credibility and exhausts patience. It, too, is a story of the Chicago slums. But *Knock on Any Door* had an impact like a right hook to the jaw. *We Fished All Night* fails completely to convince. Its principal characters are not believable. And they are dull. Rarely has a case of "second-novel trouble" been more serious. But Mr. Motley's setback is not necessarily fatal.

He has demonstrated that he has substantial talents, that he knows intimately the sordid life of which he writes, that he can tell a crudely powerful story. In spite of the failure of his second novel, his enlistment in the naturalist forces should be heartening to their depleted ranks.

If the naturalists are on doubtful ground philosophically, they are even more easily refuted by direct observation and statistics. No one in his senses would deny that poverty and ignorance, vice and crime make poor soil for growing minds. They are dreadful handicaps in life. But one has only to look around him to see that most men and women who endure such handicaps do not succumb to them, do not become degenerates and criminals. Most of them struggle hard to keep body and soul together, to hold jobs and raise families. They do not usually enjoy a fair share of the world's pleasures and rewards. But they remain abreast of the run of humanity. For every Al Capone there is an Al Smith. For every jailbird there are many decent husbands and fathers.

It is this balance which is lacking in most naturalist fiction, the balance of strong against weak, of respectable against criminal. Both are part of life in every environment. We may never know the exact proportion; but in any large group we do know that both good and bad will be found. And in recent years several writers who know as much about life in the slums as the Farrells and Wrights have written novels much more objective than theirs. Notable among these are two women, Maritta Wolff and Betty Smith.

Maritta Wolff is the precocious and prodigiously talented young woman who burst upon the American literary scene in 1941 with a first novel about the seamy side of life in Michigan, *Whistle Stop*. Miss Wolff was only twenty-two at the time, as harshly realistic and accurate an observer of underprivileged Americans as James Farrell. She was not then, and after two more books, *Night Shift* and *About Lyddy Thomas,* she still isn't the self-conscious artist type. Her contagious human warmth, her exuberant narrative drive and her prodigal richness of invention insure that her novels are magnetically alive and furiously good reading. But they also lead Miss Wolff into excessive melodramatics and so preoccupy her that she always leaves several minor characters without adequate motivation.

Nevertheless, her three novels are a substantial achievement. No contemporary American writer has a better ear for the American language as it is actually spoken on factory assembly lines, in barrooms and bus stations, shops and tenements. The pungent, ill-educated, colloquial speech of her characters is always effortlessly natural. It is no imitation, no stunt worked up by a condescending author. It is the simple, jerky, vulgar, lively talk about clothes and jobs and babies and weather and sex which Americans talk. "Leave us not be dopes, huh," says Lyddy, expressing her determination to keep her chin up, to keep fighting, and expressing it in exactly the right words.

Maritta Wolff is as tough and unrelenting in her emphasis on poverty and struggle, on violence and brutality, as any American now writing. How any girl so young could know what she knows is a source of constant astonishment. Her books are pitiful and sordid. But they are not petrified by naturalistic pessimism. Her stories quiver with physical high spirits. Some of her characters are weaklings and some are vicious. But others are kind, loyal and generous. Miss Wolff writes of them with the affection of one who sincerely and unaffectedly likes people for their own sake. And so, although her novels are sometimes shocking, they are also likable. Because of all the bustle and excitement and confusion of daily living which she crowds into them, they are continuously entertaining.

And they contain more than the usual quota of "social significance." Maritta Wolff has recognized a vitally important sector of our society for what it really is: the poor but not downtrodden factory workers and their wives, who never think or feel like "proletarians." Her characters are all too busy fighting to solve their various problems, to work out their own destinies in terms of jobs and families and love, to feel like anything save Americans.

Maritta Wolff has not yet mastered the artistic self-discipline which would enable her to prune her novels of some of their excesses, to keep them on a stable level of effectiveness, instead of seesawing between magnificent scenes and mediocre ones. But she has written of typical, lower-class American life with authority, objective understanding and fiery skill. With greater maturity and more careful editing of her work, she may become a writer of major stature. So far she has not yet received the critical attention she deserves nor has she won the public popularity which someday will inevitably be hers.

The opposite is true of Betty Smith, whose first novel, *A Tree Grows in Brooklyn,* won considerable critical success and fabulous public acclaim. Few books of our time have been so hugely popular or deserved their popularity as much. After all, most really spectacular best sellers are without literary distinction of any kind.

A Tree Grows in Brooklyn is not without flaws. It is not destined for immortality. But it does provide a rich reading experience. It is honest and true and moving and entertaining. It is a marvelously sane and well-balanced excursion into the lower depths of poverty in the slums of Brooklyn.

A Tree Grows in Brooklyn is a poignant and tenderly understanding story of childhood and family relationships as experienced by one of the most desperately poor families in a great city's desperately poorest section, the Williamsburg district of Brooklyn. It is primarily the story of the growing up and beginning of wisdom of a little girl, Francie Nolan. Francie is a superb feat of characterization, an imaginative, alert, resourceful and lovable child.

Equally triumphant characterizations are scattered all through Miss Smith's book: of Francie's charming, ineffectual, alcoholic father; of her heroically enduring mother; of her outrageously raffish and comically surprising aunt. Betty Smith knows her characters, likes them and seems to capture their vital essences on paper with effortless ease. She also is blessed with natural narrative power, the old-fashioned gift of storytelling. These qualities made *A Tree Grows in Brooklyn* enjoyable and popular.

But what made it important was Miss Smith's ability to paint a grim and unsparingly detailed picture of the lower depths without losing sight of the variety of human character, of the courage, love and loyalty which can be found wherever people are. Miss Smith did not prettify her subject. She emphasized the awful economies of rock-bottom poverty, the hunger and lacerated pride, the brutal surroundings in schools and streets which breed precocious maturity and worldliness in tenement children. She omitted nothing, no unsavory detail, neither the squalor, the vulgarity nor the suffering.

Yet in this most miserable of environments Miss Smith found laughter and courage, ambition and self-respect. The great American epic of upward progress toward education, freedom and accomplishment was still going on, handicapped by horrible difficulties, but still vital. *A Tree Grows in Brooklyn* is an intimately authoritative report on urban poverty in America written by a woman who knows that courage and honor and humor can, and do, do much to overcome the destructive forces of evil circumstance. It would have been an even better book than it is if an arbitrarily happy ending for Francie's mother were not attached by main force to its last part.

Miss Smith's sound craftsmanship and understanding heart were equally in evidence in her second novel, *Tomorrow Will Be Better*. A simpler, shorter, starker book, this sadly bitter story of the blasted hopes of two young people in the same Williamsburg slums seems to have been written to answer the critics who had objected to the sentimentality of *A Tree Grows in Brooklyn's* conclusion. As a story of hardship, worry, failure and nagging poverty *Tomorrow Will Be Better* is expert and eloquent. It is the other side of the picture, Brooklyn without the tree, without the vitality, laughter and unconquerable gal-

[48]

lantry of spirit. It is about doomed, dreary and pathetic people; but their troubles are not exclusively caused by their environment. Some come from deep within themselves. Unfortunately *Tomorrow Will Be Better* is somewhat handicapped by Miss Smith's failure to make the sexual obsession of one of her two central characters convincing.

Nevertheless, if Betty Smith's second novel is less impressive than her first, it is still the work of a gifted writer who has written with skill and power of the life she herself once knew in heartbreakingly difficult years. Miss Smith has shown in her two books how some strong and gifted characters can defy it, and also how less gifted characters succumb. And she has shown how various are individual responses to it—as various as the individual characters concerned. And even the sentimental ending of *A Tree Grows in Brooklyn* can be interpreted as a frank admission that luck, too, plays its important role in the Brooklyn slums, as it does everywhere else.

IV

SQUANDERED TALENTS:

Lewis, Steinbeck, Hemingway, O'Hara

"Every man takes the limits of his own field of vision for the limits of the world."—*Schopenhauer*

The books we have just discussed are marked by a certain clarity of purpose. Their authors hold definite opinions about politics or man's fate, and they have expressed them in fictional form. All of them may not have added a cubit to their own intellectual stature, but at least they have taken thought in a responsible and intelligent fashion. As much cannot be said for the muddled and irresponsible ideas and the debased version of human character which have undermined the recent works of John Steinbeck, John O'Hara, Sinclair Lewis and Ernest Hemingway.

These are great names in the republic of modern letters and the men who bear them are greatly talented. All of them save Mr. O'Hara are world-famous. The late Sinclair Lewis was the most celebrated American writer of this century, a Nobel Prize winner, a novelist whose achievements will never be forgotten, whose influence was incalculable. Ernest Hemingway is probably the second most celebrated modern American writer, a master literary technician whose methods have been imitated by countless lesser men. Mr. Steinbeck and Mr. O'Hara are not of comparable rank, but they, too, loom large on the American literary scene.

Even the fondest admirers of these four leading American writers do not claim that the books which they wrote during the last ten years are of major importance. To me, most of them seem unworthy of serious consideration as examples of the art of fiction. And I do not believe that the segment of the modern mind which they represent is a large or significant one as yet. But there is the possibility that the immense prestige and vast popularity of their novels may be helping to debase the modern mind of the near future. People whose ideas of life and character are influenced by a *Cannery Row* or *A Rage to Live* are that much nearer collapse into flabby cynicism, moral nihilism and tired misanthropy.

The literary phenomenon these four men represent is a depressing one: the combination of exceptional literary abilities with an exceptionally narrow outlook on life. All four are sensitive, observant, accomplished professional craftsmen in fiction. The writing skills which they have mastered deserve sincere admiration.

But they have recently turned those skills to cheap and meretricious ends: to caricature and defamation of their fellow citizens (Lewis in *Cass Timberlane*), to sentimental glorification of subhuman behavior (Mr. Steinbeck in *Cannery Row*), to a celebration of motiveless promiscuity (Mr. O'Hara in *A Rage to Live*), and to a ludicrous orgy of false values and phony emotions (Mr. Hemingway in *Across the River and into the Trees*). These books do not represent a debatable vision of life so much as the absence of one. They are filled with their authors' emotions rather than with their ideas—which wouldn't be so questionable if the emotions weren't hate, envy, scorn, bravado and a sort of biological sentimentality. And the hate does not seem to be the righteous wrath of indignation, only the yammering snarl of jangled neuroses.

The naturalists and even the proletarian writers take mankind seriously, although they hold low opinions of mankind's capacities. Perhaps these writers do also. But it is hard to believe so, because of the primitive and even debased attributes of character which they seem to respect and admire. Fools and knaves abound; weaklings and degenerates infest this planet. But they will not inherit the earth and there is no good reason why they should inherit the kingdom of fiction.

An author's right to choose his own material, to select his own characters, is absolute. But the reader, it seems to me, has an equal right to demand that if a novelist writes of hateful, depraved or criminal characters he do so seriously; that he write about the whys and wherefores, the psychological and environmental forces, which made his characters vicious or criminal. To populate a book with scoundrels and to emphasize their repeated crimes and sins without making the scoundrels interesting and important representatives of one kind of unfortunate human behavior is a sterile performance indeed. The murderous hero of Dostoevski's *Crime and Punishment* is an eternally fascinating character, because we are allowed to penetrate so far into his tormented mind. But the heroine of Mr. O'Hara's *A Rage to Live* is only dull and promiscuous because her transgressions are itemized but her mind is left nearly blank.

That Sinclair Lewis' last five novels are sadly inferior to the great ones he wrote in the 1920s cannot detract from the importance of his life achievement. From 1920 and the publication of *Main Street* until his death in 1951 this redheaded man with his deeply furrowed forehead, his freckled, haggard face, his pale-blue eyes and manner of desperate high tension, meant American literature to much of the world. His books were widely read wherever people read books at all. His passionate feeling for his native land—a white-hot compound of fierce affection and raging hatred for its vulgarities, hypocrisies and general lack of perfection—caused many of his books to be misunderstood. For seldom have they portrayed typical Americans, as many Europeans and too many Americans thought that they did.

Rather, they concentrated the distilled essence of some aspect of America and magnified it, exaggerated it, interpreted it and explained it until the nation and the world had new myths which would never be forgotten. So, as Paul Bunyan means lumberjacks and Uncle Tom slavery, George F. Babbitt has come to mean a familiar type of American businessman.

In the great books which made him famous, *Main Street, Babbitt, Arrowsmith* and *Dodsworth,* Lewis wrote with such intensity and vigor, such rampaging high spirits and satiric wit that he soared triumphantly over his own limitations, his two-dimensional characters and the repetitious exaggeration of his mocking dialogue. He was a true creator, an artist who could impose his vision of his fellow men on much of the world and make his elementary characters seem brilliantly true and more than life-sized. It was a great achievement. The former pulp-magazine editor from Sauk Center, Minnesota, had more substantial qualifications for the Nobel Prize in literature than any of the other Americans who also have won that accolade.

But the novels which Lewis wrote in the last decade of his life were either pale imitations of his earlier work or venomous outbursts of hatred and melodrama. They made a dreary conclusion to a great career. It is always a melancholy spectacle when a richly gifted writer exhausts his material or his creative abilities and continues to write anyway because writing is his life and he cannot stop while life endures. Sinclair Lewis' last five novels were: *Gideon Planish, Cass Timberlane, Kingsblood Royal, The God-Seeker* and *World So Wide.* Three of these were limp and soggy, but comparatively harmless, examples of Lewis in decline. Two, and they were much the most popular, were neurotic cries of hate.

The inoffensive ones require little comment. *Gideon Planish* was the best of the three, a moderately lively blast at the uplift racket, philanthropic foundations, pressure groups and money-raising combines. "Now get this," said Gideon. "To be realistic, I must admit that the first purpose of any uplift organization must be to support the executives who give their time and good hard work to it." If any money was left over for the allegedly worthy purpose of the organization that was just a secondary afterthought. Lewis was as angry and brutally sarcastic when he wrote *Gideon Planish* as at any time in his career. But somehow his heavy artillery sounded like popguns and his sanctimonious and hypocritical hero remained dull and insipid.

The God-Seeker was Lewis' only historical novel, the story of a Presbyterian mission to the Sioux Indians and the early days of the city of St. Paul. Its hero is a young carpenter from the Berkshires who mistakenly thought for a few years that he had a call to be a missionary. As a novel by Sinclair Lewis *The God-Seeker* is flat, dull and third-rate. Even as one of hundreds of historical novels about the American frontier published at about the same time it is mediocre.

World So Wide, his last and twenty-second novel, tells of a young man's search for knowledge of his true self in travel and in historical and artistic scholarship. In a way it reflects Lewis' own lifelong pursuit of happiness and the meaning of life, the quest which made him a restless and lonely wanderer, always moving on from one home to another, destined in the end to die, like so many other literary exiles, in Rome. If Lewis had turned his stony glare inward on his own tormented mind and written an autobiography he could have produced an important and psychologically fascinating work. But he preferred to write of a young widower discovering the bloody splendor of Italy's spectacular past, wavering between love for two rather wooden and ridiculous young women. *World So Wide* contains flashes of the old Lewis satiric gusto, but not many. On the whole it is dull and superficial.

In *Cass Timberlane* and *Kingsblood Royal* Lewis seemed to turn on the American citizens, whom he had formerly loved while he chastised them, in a fit of contemptuous rage. Satire was replaced by denunciation, understanding by spite. Prejudice and sour bad temper ran riot. The two books were not only inferior as fiction, they were cruelly unjust caricatures of American life.

Cass Timberlane is a novel about marriage, about one marriage in particular and a dozen others in general. The particular one is between a middle-aged judge, a decent, likable man something like Sam Dodsworth, and Jinny, a pretty, vivacious, selfish, stupid, unfaithful girl of twenty-one. Jinny in many respects is a reincarnation of our old friend, the child bride. The story of the ups and downs of their unhappy marriage is routine and undistinguished fare intermittently brightened by Lewis' photographic eye for the surface details of American life, by outbursts of savage wit and even by surprising interludes of whimsy and pathos. But, since a marriage with a twenty-year age difference between the contracted parties is not typical, Lewis set down his ideas on American marriage in general in a series of portrait sketches of other couples in Cass's and Jinny's circle of friends.

These comprise as ghastly a set of grossly exaggerated caricatures as Lewis could imagine. Nearly all the marriages are bitterly unhappy; the happy ones are between near idiots. Snobs, boors, drunkards, lechers, weaklings, selfish and contemptible women, vile and repulsive men, the married couples of *Cass Timberlane* draw out their sordid and petty lives in boredom and futility, occasionally enlivened by cheap and nasty adulteries. Through long stretches of this curious book the prevailing emotion seems to be pure hatred of men and women as such. The satire is gross and malicious, the cards wickedly stacked. There isn't one honorable, intelligent, loyal and affectionate couple in the whole book to relieve the monotony of blighted lives.

Somehow, somewhere, Lewis had lost his sense of balance and proportion. Divorce statistics prove that unhappy marriages are common; one eye half open is enough to find evidence that the world is not inhabited solely by the virtuous and noble. If Lewis had confined his attention to one unsavory marriage, or to three or four, all would have been well. But when he deliberately wrote of more than a dozen miserable marriages and included not one good one in the lot he passed the boundaries of reasonable satire. For artistic verisimilitude he should have remembered that, as it takes all kinds of people to make a world, so it takes all kinds of marriages to make that general abstraction, marriage. *Cass Timberlane* is so vicious a diatribe that it is neither good fiction nor effective satire.

When Lewis said of *Kingsblood Royal* that "the story itself is the important thing" he was either willfully obtuse or even more sarcastic than usual. For the story of *Kingsblood Royal* is the crudest sort of melodrama, artificial and wildly unconvincing. The only important thing about this book is its significance as Lewis' contribution to the mounting tide of protest against race discrimination. But even as propaganda for social and economic justice for Negroes, *Kingsblood Royal* is inferior. Lewis protested much too much.

In his desire to strike a blow in a good cause and in his hatred of injustice Lewis painted his canvas solely in blacks and whites and bloody reds, piled caricature on top of exaggeration, and populated his scene with a fantastic collection of detestable human skunks. His incredible plot, with his conventional hero discovering that he is one thirty-secondth Negro and his consequent involvement in persecution and riots, is an insult to credibility. How so experienced a writer with so wide an acquaintance of men and life and books could have committed this monstrosity passes all understanding. Lewis seemed to have fared beyond the realms of observation, humor, satire and artistic fiction into the dark outer marches of scurrilous propaganda.

The novels which have most effectively dramatized the Negro's plight as a second-class citizen have made their points by arousing sympathy for unhappy people without making monsters out of other people, equally human, who accept the inequalities of segregation and discrimination customary in their social culture. Environment, as was admitted earlier, is a powerful force. It always pushes people toward conformity, although it cannot rob them of their power to choose on issues which matter to them. The crux of the race problem is that the misfortunes of others rarely matter much to most people.

In *Kingsblood Royal* Lewis ignored such considerations and

[57]

portrayed his hero's former friends as gibbering Nazis, ardent believers in every slander ever circulated against Negroes, and even argumentatively convinced that Negroes "would be a damn sight better off under slavery."

It just didn't wash. The Negro-baiters of *Kingsblood Royal* are as unreal and unrepresentative as the husbands and wives of *Cass Timberlane,* and Lewis hated them with equal gusto. Race prejudice undoubtedly flourishes in Minnesota as well as in Georgia, but it varies from person to person in the degree of its virulence and all the prejudiced are not monsters. Lewis, by abandoning all restraint in his plea for tolerance, did more to increase the world's excess of hate than he did to diminish it. His warm feeling for average Americans had degenerated into irrational contempt. Sinclair Lewis' last two really popular books were completely unworthy of the author of *Arrowsmith.*

And such lapses are inevitable, for writers cannot be expected to maintain unfailing standards of excellence. Even Shakespeare wrote *Cymbeline* as well as *Hamlet.* Robert Southey was realistic and sensible when he said that writers who hoped to live by their profession must publish anything they can get into print, knowing that they will be remembered only by their best work. Writers are not judged by the average of their total output, but by their maximum achievements.

Mark Antony's famous words of gloom in his funeral oration for Caesar,

> "The evil that men do lives after them;
> The good is oft interred with their bones . . ."

frequently apply to the ideas and influence of writers, but rarely to the literary immortality of specific books. A writer's reputation depends on his finest books. John Steinbeck's depends on *The Grapes of Wrath.*

Although Mr. Steinbeck's first novel was published as early as 1929, he did not receive much attention until the appearance of his fourth, *Tortilla Flat,* in 1935. *The Grapes of Wrath,* his greatest popular as well as critical success, came in 1939. That bitter and eloquent story of the sufferings of migratory farm laborers in the trough of the depression moved the heart of the nation. Since then Mr. Steinbeck's whole career has consisted of one long anticlimax.

Technically, *The Grapes of Wrath* was a proletarian novel, a furious blast at social injustice. But Mr. Steinbeck's skill in creative characterization, in making the members of his Oakie family, the Joads, intensely human and pitifully interesting, added to its social protest the extra dimension of art. The magnificent courage of Ma Joad made her one of the unforgettable characters of American fiction.

The Grapes of Wrath is so greatly superior to anything else Mr. Steinbeck has done that it almost conveys the false impression that its creator is a one-book writer. But there were seven Steinbeck books before it, two of them good (*Of Mice and Men* and *The Red Pony*), and there have been nine since. Of these only one, an Indian folk tale called *The Pearl,* has any claim to distinction. The rest are a curious grab bag of literary odds and ends.

In *The Forgotten Village* Mr. Steinbeck wrote the text to a picture book about life in a Mexican Indian village. In *Sea of Cortez* he wrote about the marine life of the gulf of California and his own none-too-clear brooding on men and mollusks and the biological meaning of life. One gathered that Mr. Steinbeck preferred mollusks to many men. *The Moon Is Down* was a play barely disguised in fiction form, about Norway under German occupation. It was slight and unimpressive. In addition to these Mr. Steinbeck also wrote about the air force, *Bombs Away,* as a contribution to the war effort, and a book about a trip to Russia, *A Russian Journal,* as a contribution to international understanding.

Four novels remain to be considered, the books which are the evidence of the decline of John Steinbeck as a novelist of major significance. Two of these are monumental examples of utter intellectual confusion, *Cannery Row* and *The Wayward Bus.* Two are examples of Mr. Steinbeck's groping for some kind of affirmative faith in men. One of them, *The Pearl,* is good in the primitive, elementary fashion of its folk theme. The other, *Burning Bright,* is a plea for the basic virtues of love and loyalty in human relations (and therefore a refreshing improvement on the moral morass of *Cannery Row* and *The Wayward Bus*); but it is sloppy, sentimental and awkwardly artificial.

In *Cannery Row* Mr. Steinbeck did not just write a trivial and seemingly meaningless and purposeless novel. He wrote, with all his usual professional felicity of expression, a sentimental glorification of weakness of mind and degeneration of character. The general atmosphere is one of biological benevolence, a sort of beaming approbation for human activities conducted below the demarcation line of pride, honesty, self-respect and minimum decency. In many of his earlier books Mr. Steinbeck had previously demonstrated his love and admiration for simple-minded people whose intelligence and standards of conduct were rudimentary at best. But in *Cannery Row* he allowed his condescending affection to boil over into sentimentality, pathos and even whimsy.

Mr. Steinbeck's bums had "no families, no money and no

ambitions beyond food, drink and contentment." They were lazy, dishonest, drunken and useless. They lied and stole. They got drunk and wrecked the property of their best friend. They had no redeeming qualities, no charm, no courage, not even a wan little good intention. Mr. Steinbeck admired them enormously and seemed to consider them the salt of the earth. Why is beyond comprehension, since Mr. Steinbeck did not even bother to characterize his bums and endow them with individual personalities.

If *Cannery Row* were only feeble and foolish as a novel, it could be dismissed at once to the limbo of bad books where it belongs. But it is not just a bad book. Mr. Steinbeck did not write seriously about the shriveled minds and maggoty characters of his bums. He was not even content to tell some faintly amusing anecdotes about them and let it go at that. He insisted with deliberate perversity on exalting his bums, on conveying the impression that they were lovable and admirable, that their way of life without ideas or ideals, without love or loyalty, without purpose or effort, was charming and attractive. Intellectual and moral confusion could go no further. But it could be matched, and was, in *The Wayward Bus*.

The Wayward Bus is a vulgar and superficial novel, a tired and tiresome reworking of a shopworn formula, the arbitrary throwing together of a group of strangers into a common danger so that each of them may reveal his character under stress. The characters isolated by a bus accident in *The Wayward Bus* are socially several cuts above the worthless riffraff of *Cannery Row*. But Mr. Steinbeck's fond affection for the social pariahs of his earlier book is here replaced by a sort of contemptuous pity. The marooned passengers of his novel are all crude caricatures of familiar types. Weak, bitter, unhappy and frustrated,

[61]

they are haunted by the biological facts of life. Sex preys on their minds with tedious monotony.

If this were the only point made in *The Wayward Bus* one could conclude that Mr. Steinbeck had attempted some kind of satire, ill conceived and splenetic though it is. Perhaps he did. But there is a further interpretation inherent in the theme of *The Wayward Bus*.

All but two of the characters in this grotesque parable of American life are petty weaklings. The two exceptions are "the blonde," whose beauty and kinetic sexuality make it impossible for her to hold an ordinary job, who earns her living sitting without clothes in giant wineglasses at stag smokers; and the bus driver, a capable, self-confident, kindly fellow bursting with animal vitality. Neither "the blonde" nor the bus driver is an admirable character; but they both are greatly superior in courage and intelligence to all the others. It might be a coincidence. But it is hard to escape the conclusion that Mr. Steinbeck is saying that intelligence and courage depend on animal strength and sexual magnetism. Bernarr MacFadden said the same thing in *Physical Culture Magazine* for thirty years.

To turn from the fetid atmosphere of *Cannery Row* and *The Wayward Bus* to the artful simplicity and emotional power of *The Pearl* is an intellectual shock. One wonders how the same author could have written them at about the same time. *The Pearl* is a Mexican Indian folk tale which Mr. Steinbeck heard on the Lower California peninsula. It is as stark and simple as folk literature generally is. And it is permeated with the special sort of impotent and sullen bitterness which only an oppressed and subject people know. This may be why it attracted Mr. Steinbeck.

For much of his life he has written about simple, childlike

and fairly primitive people. His preoccupation with them seems to have been a conscious protest against the decadence, cruelty and stupidity which have been so prevalent in this century among so-called civilized and advanced peoples. So when Mr. Steinbeck wrote of the gay and irresponsible paysanos of *Tortilla Flat* he struck a note which appealed to many readers. But when he waxed enthusiastic over the debased bums of *Cannery Row* he seemed not to be praising the natural man, but to be denying the essential human decencies, to be finding life best when lived on a merely biological level.

In *The Pearl* Mr. Steinbeck wrote about genuinely primitive people, illiterate, superstitious Indian fishermen. But they were primitive without being debased. They were altogether admirable in their love and loyalty, pride and ambition, hope and fear. Their sufferings were of the spirit, not just of the flesh, and so their misfortunes are universally significant and not just pitiful.

One of the characteristic symptoms of decadence in the modern mind is flight from the tension and terror of Western civilization into the simpler world of primitive societies. Many writers who profess to loathe New York as if it were Babylon have written books about the joy and peace and spiritual solace to be found among Eskimos, Balinese, Arabs and Indians. Mr. Steinbeck hasn't gone quite so far; but it is interesting that the only impressive book he has written since *The Grapes of Wrath* is about basic emotions and eternal values in the lives of simple Indians.

The actual story of *The Pearl* is a parable about the evil loosed among men by hope of vast wealth symbolized by a fabulous pearl. It is a simple and direct story with no subtleties of characterization or profundities of thought. Yet its impact is

[63]

powerful. The Indian father who fought that his son might have a better chance than he is an heroic figure. His devotion to his family and his courage in the face of death are deeply moving. They give *The Pearl* a timeless and universally human appeal, for they are virtues which men everywhere have always admired.

Still on the side of the angels (but much less effectively) was *Burning Bright,* Mr. Steinbeck's third play in fiction form. Artificial, peculiar and rigidly symbolical, *Burning Bright* is a moral lesson celebrating the virtues of love and loyalty and courage. As a novel it is mediocre. Its characters are unbelievable wooden puppets. The dialogue they are forced to speak is painfully stylized, sometimes sounding like a parody of *Hiawatha.* But, in spite of its preposterous artificialities, *Burning Bright* manages to be mildly interesting.

The reading mind can quickly adjust itself to the most bizarre literary conventions. When they are employed to dramatize a simple story about basic emotions involved in the eternal triangle something human comes through, even if the characters have no life or interest in themselves. *Burning Bright* is not an impressive performance and it is sentimental. But then much of Mr. Steinbeck's work has been sentimental. The important thing is that in his last two novels he has at least been sentimental about people and qualities worthy of respect. Whether he can regain the high rank he held among American writers after the publication of *The Grapes of Wrath* the future will tell. But he has at least climbed out of the pitfall represented by *Cannery Row* and *The Wayward Bus.*

Just as it was necessary in discussing Sinclair Lewis' recent books to remember *Babbitt* and *Arrowsmith* and in considering the recent work of John Steinbeck to keep *The Grapes of Wrath* in mind, so it is essential in writing of Ernest Hemingway's *Across the River and into the Trees* to place it in proper perspective with Mr. Hemingway's total output. And if literary justice (that unattainable ideal surrounded by barbed-wire entanglements of prejudice and opinion) is to be approached, some brief tribute must be paid to Mr. Hemingway's spectacular achievements in the past, even though only one of his books was published in the last decade, which is our principal concern in these pages.

Ever since the publication of *The Sun Also Rises* in 1926, Ernest Hemingway's star has flamed like a spectacular and baleful comet across our literary skies. Hemingway the rampant individualist has been almost as ardently admired, pettishly disliked and avidly discussed as Hemingway the writer. His manner and matter have been more widely imitated by younger writers than those of any of his contemporaries. Mr. Hemingway's celebrated characters plod like zombies through hundreds of mediocre books by lesser, would-be Hemingways. Echoes of his personal style reverberate in hundreds of other forgotten books. *A Farewell to Arms* is not only a good novel about the First World War; it is *the* American novel of that war. *For Whom the Bell Tolls* is not only a fine novel about the Spanish civil war; it is *the* American novel about war and fascism and the fateful political issues of the 1930s.

Although I am tempted to write still another extensive treatise on the life and works of Ernest Hemingway, I must content myself here with a few comments on Mr. Hemingway's world and Mr. Hemingway's technique. His world is uniquely his own, a small segment of the twentieth-century world. It is a world of unparalleled violence born of the horrors of the First World War and the intellectual and spiritual disillusionment which followed it. Most of its inhabitants lead a life of sensation only, usually mistaking sexual desire for love, devoting themselves to excitement rather than positive achievement. Uninterested in ideas or ideals, they value courage above all other virtues and admire physical skills more than any other accomplishments, particularly when skill and courage can be combined in one activity such as in bullfighting or lion hunting. The joys of food, drink, sport and fornication are their preoccupation because they are haunted by the specter of death. Mr. Hemingway called his book on bullfighting *Death in the Afternoon;* but death is imminent for twenty-four hours a day in all his work. It is the unstated theme of his greatest short stories, "The Killers," "The Short Happy Life of Francis Macomber" (complicated by cowardice) and "The Snows of Kilimanjaro." To face death with courage is the supreme human virtue in the universe of Ernest Hemingway. Those who have not faced it, preferably in battle, are demonstrably inferior human beings.

Ernest Hemingway has never been a thoughtful writer. His peculiar vision of life does not seem to be the result of conscious reflection, but of an intense emotional response. And his brutal, animalistic world has chilled and repelled many readers. If he only admired something beyond the capacity of a professional gladiator! It was the new (for Mr. Hemingway) factor of belief in *For Whom the Bell Tolls* which gave that uneven but magnificent novel its unquestioned rank as his finest book. For the first time he seemed to have found a cause worthy of his allegiance, the cause of freedom in arms against fascism and threatened from the rear by communism.

Mr. Hemingway's world, alas, is undeniably a recognizable part of the modern world. And as time passes and current news becomes past history the segment of the modern world it reflects grows. The growth may be as unhealthy as that of a cancerous tumor and as dangerous, but it cannot be denied. Moral restraints have lost their power to control a large percentage of humanity. The cult of violence gains new converts every day.

It is, perhaps, the most curious aspect of Mr. Hemingway's success in capturing the imagination of many thousands of readers that he did so by conveying an atmosphere and expressing a primitive attitude, not by creating memorable individual characters. There are few characters in his fiction who stick in the memory as particular human beings, or even as significant types. We remember the cynical picture of war in *A Farewell to Arms* and the oddly sentimentalized wartime love affair. But the hero, Lieutenant Henry, is only a gray shadow and the heroine is only an old passion clothed in a nurse's uniform.

The hero of *For Whom the Bell Tolls* is equally inert, and the unfortunate heroine is better remembered for her cropped hair and her participation in the famous and ludicrous sleeping-bag episode than as a special person. What was her name now? It is the guerrilla chieftain's wife, the superwoman Pilar, who alone survives in memory and who will continue to do so as long as the bitter courage and heroic defiance of the Spanish people in the civil war are not forgotten. Pilar is Mr. Hemingway's only triumphant feat of characterization.

We return, then, to his brilliant fictional technique, his dialogue consisting of short, concrete statements, his concentration on the physical world of things and the physical world of violent action, his passionate search for the exact word which will express an exact and limited truth, his experiments with prose rhythms which have transformed the staccato rattle of his early writing into the liquid, cadenced ripple of some of his later work. The truth is that Ernest Hemingway is a stylist and a fine one. He is also a poet. His sensitivity to the light, color, form and atmosphere of particular places is lyrical; his ability to suggest an emotional atmosphere (usually of an elementary sort) is remarkable. Mr. Hemingway is unquestionably a master literary craftsman. What his mind can conceive his typewriter will transfer to paper with superb skill.

It is what his mind conceived, or failed to conceive, which is the ruination of *Across the River and into the Trees.* This short novel was published in 1950, ten years after *For Whom the Bell Tolls.* The long gap is partly explained by Mr. Hemingway's preoccupation with the Second World War, in which he served for a while as a newspaper correspondent, and partly by his application to a much longer and more ambitious novel which he laid aside in order to write *Across the River and into the Trees.*

Nevertheless, a gap of ten years in Mr. Hemingway's literary output, the years between the ages of forty-one and fifty-one which should be the most productive and fruitful in a major writer's career, seems an odd development in the life of a man so obviously born to write. And then to break his long silence with a novel as disappointing as *Across the River and into the Trees* raises nasty doubts. Have Mr. Hemingway's powers declined as much as this, or is this just another inevitable mistake by the man who wrote the inferior *To Have and Have Not* and followed it up with the stunning *For Whom the Bell Tolls?*

Across the River and into the Trees is a postwar love story laid in Venice. Its protagonists are an American army colonel of fifty-one and an Italian countess of nineteen. The colonel is in danger of death at any minute from a heart condition and he knows it. So he drinks beyond the capacity of mortal man to consume alcohol and retain powers of speech, talks interminably to his young mistress, who can never hear enough of his reminiscences, opinions and spiteful prejudices, and makes vigorous love in gondolas and hotel rooms.

The colonel is real enough as a callous, boastful, spiteful, self-pitying buffoon. But the countess is as unreal as a girl on a billboard advertisement. Her only attributes are beauty, aristocracy, amorous passion and patient curiosity to know more of the colonel's deplorable opinions. Instead of seeming like a flesh-and-blood human being she seems like a high-school sophomore's dream girl.

The countess is a fictional failure; but the love affair is worse than a failure. It is silly and ludicrous. When the colonel calls his mistress "daughter" one's skin crawls with a sort of literary embarrassment. When the countess says, "Love me true," one shudders at such a distortion of human speech. The result is painful and sad. Mr. Hemingway has failed in the basic first step of fiction: to persuade, to convince, to make his characters real enough so that his readers may temporarily believe in them. If this first step is not achieved successfully there is no possibility of taking the second, which is to make the characters seem interesting and significant as well as believable.

But *Across the River and into the Trees* is not just a poor novel. It is a novel which seems highly questionable in its basic assumptions. It is nearly impossible for a novelist to conceal his private opinion of his characters. And it is plain that Mr. Hemingway does not only sympathize with his colonel; he also admires him. Now the colonel, it seems to me, has only

[69]

one admirable quality, his courage. Save for that, he is thoroughly obnoxious, a bully and a braggart, a surly egoist who patronizes or snubs his inferiors and sneers at his superiors.

Admirers of *Across the River and into the Trees* (there are a few) may claim that the colonel is all these things because he is a serious psychological study of a man emotionally crippled by war, embittered by a demotion in rank, befuddled by love and tense with the strain of imminent death. Such an interpretation is a generous recognition of Mr. Hemingway's possible intention. But to my mind the evidence is not there in cold type. The colonel actually found in these pages is a brutal egoist ridiculously miscast in the role of a tragic lover. Such men undoubtedly exist. But to romanticize them with false glamour is an exercise in a sort of perverse sentimentality.

It remains to admit that *Across the River and into the Trees* is not a total failure. Mr. Hemingway's old magic comes through in sudden flashes, chiefly in re-creating the atmosphere of Venice and in describing a duck-hunting expedition in the marshes of the Adriatic. Mr. Hemingway, even at his weakest, can still arrange words in uniquely exciting patterns. He is a true artist who has lapsed and recovered before. Everyone interested in modern literature sincerely hopes that his next book will be as superior to *Across the River and into the Trees* as *For Whom the Bell Tolls* was to *To Have and Have Not*.

The strange case of John O'Hara has several resemblances to Mr. Hemingway's, although on a much smaller scale, for Mr. O'Hara is an exceedingly minor writer while Mr. Hemingway is unquestionably a major one. Nevertheless, Mr. O'Hara is a technically expert craftsman in fiction, a master of colloquial dialogue, a shrewd observer of the tribal folkways and social customs of his fellow citizens. But, like Mr. Hemingway, he has limited his focus to a small portion of the human comedy, and, also like Mr. Hemingway, he has had no interpretation of life to offer, only an emotional reaction to it. Mr. O'Hara's world is populated by the cheap, vulgar, debased and self-destroyed. His reaction to it is a mixture of sardonic scorn, savage contempt and romantic wonder. When the scorn and contempt prevail, as they do in his short stories, Mr. O'Hara is at least intelligently consistent. When the romanticism runs riot and beglamours the by now notorious heroine of *A Rage to Live,* the result is an abomination, a travesty of false values and decadent sentimentality.

There are three different countries in the fictional world of John O'Hara and the record shows that Mr. O'Hara does not think much of any of them. He paid his discourteous respects to the country-club and serious-drinking set in his first novel, *Appointment in Samarra,* which was published in 1934. His second, *Butterfield 8,* was a tawdry, tedious, brutal and explicit exploration of sottish debauchery in New York during the speak-easy era. His third, *Hope of Heaven,* was about Holly-wood and a group of equally degraded characters.

In five volumes of short stories Mr. O'Hara kept the same kind of human vermin spinning on the same old merry-go-round. He did so with considerable dexterity, with cold distaste and with caustic malice. Quick diagnoses of human nature at its worst, his sarcastic but rarely humorous tales with their worm's-eye view of the underside of human character grew increasingly tiresome. Mr. O'Hara's narrow and sour outlook never had the dignity and stature of true satire. He seemed to be finding what he hunted for in American life and to be blind to, or uninterested in, everything else.

Reading the stories collected in volumes like *Pipe Night* and

Hellbox one immediately finds that Mr. O'Hara holds a low opinion of the prosperous, the successful and the fashionably educated. But in writing about economically and socially fortunate people he does not satirize them. Instead, he just seems belligerent, cross, vituperative, rather than critical because he believes in higher standards of behavior to which his victims are indifferent.

And when he came to his most ambitious work, *A Rage to Live,* he forsook even his pseudosatirical approach. This long novel is not without virtues. It does possess a vibrant vitality, a solidity and force which hold attention. Most of its characters are skillfully real; but most of them are not interesting in themselves and much of their behavior is loathsome. Mr. O'Hara itemized the nasty details of his characters' lubricous sexuality with an unnecessary offensiveness which seemed to spring more from a juvenile desire to be sensationally shocking than from any artistic need. It was tasteless cataloguing, when a judicious suggestion would have conveyed his point more artfully. Adult readers can imagine what kind of people his characters are without being taken on a conducted tour of the stews of life.

A Rage to Live is the story of Grace Caldwell Tate, the reigning society beauty of Fort Penn, a city exactly like Harrisburg, Pennsylvania. To a lesser extent it is the story of a dozen lesser characters and of Fort Penn itself. Parts of it deserve serious consideration, for there are good things in this curious novel: its complete, realistically specific and subtle analysis of the social structure of an American city, class lines and class influence, economic and political power, municipal graft and secret manipulations; its long gallery of excellent minor characters revealed in vivid flashes with each talking his own shop-talk with complete naturalness; its wonderfully adroit dialogue used to let people characterize themselves and to advance the story.

These are substantial virtues, proof that Mr. O'Hara could, if he would, achieve a literary stature he has never yet even come near. But they are vitiated by serious shortcomings. *A Rage to Live* is overstuffed, not only with furnishings, food and clothes, but also with nearly irrelevant scenes and extraneous material; its narrative pace, sometimes so crisp and sure, is all too often slow and circuitous; and its heroine is not interesting in herself and is entirely unworthy of so massive a fictional monument.

Grace Caldwell Tate was beautiful, rich and socially pre-eminent in Fort Penn. Naturally, then, she had poise and self-confidence. But she was not intelligent, not even clever. She was ruthlessly selfish and she would not, or could not, control her sexual passions. Whether Grace was a sick woman or just a promiscuous one Mr. O'Hara doesn't indicate. But he writes of her as if she were only courageously unconventional, as if she were a gallant and charming heroine. Moral confusion can go no farther. Pity is the most appropriate reaction to the Graces of this world. Indignation is understandable. But such romantic glorification is beyond understanding.

The trouble with Grace as the protagonist of a serious work of fiction, it seems to me, is that Mr. O'Hara did not endow her with genuine feeling. If she had loved greatly, or even sincerely, with any depth of emotion and real devotion, she might have been interesting. If the inner workings of her mind, the psychology which drove her to perdition, had been emphasized instead of her charm, she might have been interesting. But Grace's inability to control her sluttish impulses is not enough to make her a significant character. Her story could have been a psychological drama or a moral tragedy. As Mr. O'Hara wrote it, it was only the story of a degenerate glamour girl.

A Rage to Live, because of the gossip value of its sensationalism, sold widely. It was a great commercial success. Its significance as a work of fictional art is negligible. But its significance in the career of John O'Hara is great. It is a sad spectacle when a man of great natural gifts devotes them to such a book. What narrower or more superficial conception of life can a man have than this—to write such a story and not to see it in terms of clinical psychology or moral tragedy?

Late in the autumn of 1951 Mr. O'Hara's latest book was published, a novelette called *The Farmer's Hotel.* Using the traditional device of a hotel as a setting where people could be assembled who otherwise would never meet, Mr. O'Hara wrote with his usual skill a peculiar little parable about modern life. His characters come from three separate walks of life: the privileged and wealthy usually called "society," the lowest possible stratum of Broadway show business, and ordinary citizens of a small Pennsylvania town.

The Farmer's Hotel contains some of Mr. O'Hara's typically convincing dialogue and some neat plotting. But its interest lies in its being Mr. O'Hara's first experiment in symbolism. One can guess that his hotel stands for the modern world, and his brutal and murderous truck driver for our modern worshipers of irrational force and violence. But even though it is heartening to find Mr. O'Hara essaying something new, *The Farmer's Hotel* does not make any particularly valid point.

Nevertheless, this unpretentious little book might prove to be a major turning point in Mr. O'Hara's career. Forsaking his usual flashy and sordid themes, he at least tried to grapple with some of the major issues of our time.

[74]

V

Mann, Faulkner

"Now we see through a glass, darkly."
—*I Corinthians*

One of the most hotly debated issues in modern literature is: Is obscurity in literature justified, and if so to what degree short of blithering madness, and what is obscure anyway? This discussion has waxed and waned in intensity for a century or more, because for at least that long some of the world's greatest writers have chosen to wrap themselves and their works in a mantle of obscurity, obscurity of thought and of expression.

Browning wrote poems which he admitted only God could understand. Today T. S. Eliot writes poetry which blazes with the authentic fire of a great talent, but which few people in the world can claim to understand completely. George Meredith through most of his career and Henry James in the latter part of his wrote novels so festooned with labyrinthine coils of self-conscious rhetoric that they present formidable obstacles to their readers, but obstacles which are eminently worth surmounting.

This tendency has received additional impetus in recent years from several sources. One source is the new fields of knowledge

[75]

which are conditioning the modern mind, particularly psycho-analysis, and which are too complicated for simple expression. Another is the conviction that the reading public is now sub-divided into many sections and that one section revels in the challenge of obscurity. This is true; but that section is a small one. Another is a neurotic kind of arrogance which scorns to please or attract, which sneers at the generality of mankind baffled by its own obscurity.

Particularly influential has been the dubious example and international acclaim of James Joyce. *Finnegans Wake* may be a prodigious monument of learning, ingenuity and symbolism; but it is a monument inscribed in almost indecipherable hiero-glyphics. Since its understanding requires several years' intense application and the study of several "keys" and "commentaries," it remains only a puzzle for pundits. The colossal self-esteem which inspired Joyce to think he was justified in demanding such sacrifices from his readers is one of the literary marvels of our time.

Finnegans Wake, of course, is the *reductio ad absurdum* of literary obscurity. In his more famous and widely imitated *Ulysses* Joyce probably reached the Farthest North to which a large number of readers are willing to accompany a "difficult" writer. *Ulysses,* too, is heavy going, clogged with ambiguities, esoteric references, symbols, puns and incoherent vaporings. Nevertheless, it is also a work of genius, filled with wit and psychological insight and poetic emotion, fascinating as an experiment in fictional technique. When a novelist offers such tangible rewards there will always be readers glad to struggle through the verbal underbrush which obscures them. *Moby Dick* is not the most obvious of books, but it is a great one and greatly beloved.

[76]

The Eminently Obscure

The issue of literary obscurity is complicated by the difficulty of defining it. What is as dark as the Styx to an executive who majored in business administration in college may be as clear as spring water to a university professor of English. To insist that the novelist should write books which everyone can understand, as Tolstoy did when he advocated writing books comprehensible to Russia's moujiks (peasants), is absurd; and Tolstoy did not practice what he preached in this respect. But to write fiction so obscurely that it repels and bewilders the highly educated and widely read seems perversely purposeless. After all, all art, and particularly the art of writing, consists in the communication of ideas and emotions. When the communication is cut off from all but a corporal's guard of kindred spirits, the writer has destroyed most of his book's excuse for being.

Perhaps we may conclude that a novel is obscure when a habitual reader of the best in literature has serious difficulty in understanding it. It is my own fervently held conviction that such obscurity is intolerable unless it is compensated for by unusual merits, and that much modern obscurity is the result of foggy thinking and turgid writing. But we must remember that a degree of difficulty which demands intelligence, alert attention and considerable cultural background is not necessarily obscure. It may be a writer's wise and deliberate choice, the reflection of his personality and of his legitimate decision to address himself to a limited and cultivated audience.

Two writers, both of them extravagantly admired throughout much of the world, both of them winners of the Nobel Prize, are generally considered densely obscure, particularly by persons only slightly acquainted with their works. But many of their discriminating admirers do not agree that either

In My Opinion

Thomas Mann or William Faulkner is obscure. Others who do admit the presence of a certain fogginess in their pages insist that it is not enough to obscure normal vision, that their literary merits are so notable that their occasional failures in communication are of little consequence.

Thomas Mann is called by some "the greatest living man of letters." Others of a more temperate disposition are content to describe him as "the greatest living German writer." Without splitting hairs over such honorary titles, it must be admitted that Mr. Mann's fame, his legend and the august nimbus which surrounds him are among the most remarkable literary phenomena of our time. His great achievements in the novel and the short story, his eloquent championship of the best in German culture and civilization while most Germans were disgracing both, and the austere manner in which he frequently betrays his awareness of his own pre-eminence have combined to make him the universally acknowledged representative of German literature. No American has ever achieved such authority, although Mark Twain and Emerson came closest to it here. We must turn to Victor Hugo's prestige in France in the last century and Samuel Johnson's in England in the eighteenth to find a comparable situation.

Since 1898, when his first book, *Little Herr Friedemann,* appeared, Mr. Mann has produced an impressive body of work, novels, novelettes, short stories, critical essays and political pamphlets. But his greatest achievements, those which will insure his fame for many years to come, were all published before the last decade, which is our primary concern here. The monumental *The Magic Mountain,* one of the incontestable masterpieces of this century, was published in 1923. His best short fiction was written before 1931. During the last ten years Mr.

Mann has written several eloquent political pamphlets, collected his critical essays and short stories in definitive volumes, completed his gigantic "Joseph" series, and produced four other novels, three of them lesser works and one a major effort. Few writers have accomplished as much between the ages of sixty-five and seventy-five.

Thomas Mann is without doubt a master of literature and a profound student of the life of man. His erudition in a dozen subjects is stupendous. Although most of his work has been fiction, most of it has been devoted to subtle and analytical elaborations of his major ideas. His later novels have possessed few of the ordinary virtues of fiction. He has dissected characters rather than created them; his philosophizing has smothered his storytelling. His magisterial prose has hung like a stiff, gorgeous and frequently opaque curtain—his uneasy but respectful readers on one side and his ideas on the other.

It is an interesting factor in Mr. Mann's career that he, who is so supremely a thinker and an intellectual, should several times have ignored or misunderstood political issues. He has said of himself that he was once "a nonpolitical man." He did not take public notice of the Nazis in his native country until late in their rise to power. Eventually he spoke out nobly against them and eloquently championed the democratic cause, but his awareness of the Nazi menace came late. And even after he became an American citizen his political understanding still was so muddled that he allowed himself to be identified with several dubious causes.

Thomas Mann's five most recent novels are *The Beloved Returns: Lotte in Weimar, The Transposed Heads, Joseph the Provider, Doctor Faustus: The Life of the German Composer Adrian Leverkühn as Told by a Friend* and *The Holy Sinner.*

Joseph and *Faustus* are much the most important and ambitious, and much the densest and most difficult.

The Beloved Returns is a novel about Goethe in his old age and the visit to Weimar of the elderly lady who as a girl had inspired *The Sorrows of Werther*. Not Lotte herself, made famous by the great man's romanticism, but Goethe as a transcendent literary genius, how he affected other people and how he thought, is the principal theme of Mr. Mann's story. He has told it in an involved and artificial fashion that is psychologically profound and a brilliant tour de force.

The novel is broken arbitrarily into several distinct parts. Those most important consist of three enormously protracted conversations in which Goethe's secretary, his son and a social acquaintance analyze the genius' character and in doing so reveal their own—and of a marvelous chapter in the stream-of-consciousness technique, rendering Goethe's thoughts on awakening.

Never once is Mr. Mann quite persuasive that such one-sided and eloquent conversations could take place. Yet from them emerges a complex portrait which is utterly convincing. Goethe's own thoughts are even more impressive. They seem as if he actually thought them, and they also seem like the thoughts of a superlatively great writer. Students of the art of fiction and lovers of Goethe will pour over these pages for years. But more general readers will be justified in finding them of limited and special interest.

The Transposed Heads is a much slighter and much less successful effort, the most peculiar and least impressive of all Mr. Mann's novels. It is a legend of ancient India, the story of Sita of the beautiful hips, of the husband and friend who both loved her, and of the terrible complications which arose when the goddess Kali transposed the two men's heads to each other's bodies. Which then was the lawful husband? Written with exquisite care in a mock-heroic style, with many ironic undertones and many excursions into Hindu metaphysics, it is only a highly mannered and ponderously artificial novelette. Whether you consider it genuinely humorous or just silly probably depends on how intimidated you are by Mr. Mann's towering reputation.

Joseph the Provider is the fourth and concluding volume in Mr. Mann's massive tetralogy based upon the Biblical story of Joseph. It is 608 closely printed pages long; the entire tetralogy takes 2,011 pages. The Joseph series may be said to have two principal themes: an analysis of the egoism of a creative genius (a theme to which Mr. Mann has returned repeatedly in both his criticism and his fiction) and a treatise on the origin of religious and ethical ideas. The story of Joseph takes up only a few pages in the Book of Genesis. But around this simple, timeless fable Mr. Mann has constructed a vast and intricately complex structure.

With colossal learning in Hebrew, Greek, Babylonian and Egyptian mythology, with solemn Teutonic pedantry and with an Oriental luxuriance of imagery, an ornate and repetitious excess of words—never one where two or two hundred will do—Mr. Mann wove a brilliantly brocaded tapestry. It is amazing to see from what tiny clues in the Biblical story he deduced his subtle and complex conclusions. But the center of his interest in the Joseph series was not in telling a story, but in exploring ancient ideas of divinity, the growth of religious concepts and the development of human personality. These ideas he expounded in rapturous dialogues encrusted so thickly with symbolism that their meaning is wonderfully obscure. It is often impossible to tell just what the Joseph books are all about.

The lack of conventional narrative increases the oppressive gloom. Joseph himself is the only human character in the series; the others are mere symbols of religious or moral abstractions. There is skill, learning, and even a baroque sort of beauty in the Joseph books; but there is no breath of life. As fiction, as novels for readers who enjoy that form of literature, they are stiff, pompous and dull.

No matter how admirable the research on which they were based, no matter how profound their speculation, they are not genuine examples of creative fiction. Those who really enjoy them and are not just bowing to intellectual fashion would probably enjoy as much a publication of the American Philosophical Society, *Sumerian Mythology: A Study of Spiritual and Literary Achievement in the Third Millennium* B.C., by S. N. Kramer.

In *Doctor Faustus* Mr. Mann produced another formidable compilation of speculative thought. As a work of philosophy it is brilliant, though ponderous and stuffy. As a novel it is clumsy, stilted and woefully tedious. Only by the loosest use of the term can it be called a novel at all. Its inner core, the story of a musical genius, is hidden beneath a mass of turgid and obscure dissertations on subjects which have fascinated Mr. Mann for much of his life: the nature of artistic genius, the effect of disease on mind and character, art, culture, theology, the German national character and technical and theoretical problems of musical composition.

If such discussions were presented in a lively fashion, integrated into the story of several interesting characters, they might not prove too heavy a burden for a novel to carry. But in *Doctor Faustus* Mr. Mann concentrated on his lecturing and neglected both his story and his characterization. His composer-hero is an allegorical figure, a symbol of intellectual pride and also of the German nation. His resemblance to the lengendary Faustus and also to several actual composers and writers just serves to make him a more unreal abstraction.

As an exhibition of intellectual fireworks *Doctor Faustus* is undoubtedly awe-inspiring. No other living writer could have written it. But it is a philosophical novel with few of the virtues of more conventional fiction. The ideas it presents are not significant to the development of a character who is interesting and believable in himself. Its hero is only a pretentiously symbolical automaton, and the ideas themselves are lost among storm clouds of rolling rhetoric with only an occasional lightning flash of brilliant lucidity.

Although *The Holy Sinner* is burdened with its full share of peculiar mannerisms, it is the simplest and liveliest narrative Mr. Mann has written in many years. A medieval legend which is a variation on the Greek story of Oedipus, only with a doubly incestuous theme instead of a single one, it is Christian and romantic in spirit instead of pagan and tragic. A story of sin and repentance, of good born of monstrous evil, it is a parable with a properly edifying conclusion. But it is also an eleventh-century romance, naïve and credulous, filled with wondrous feats of arms, fantastic coincidences and numerous miracles.

For modern readers so fanciful a parable is hard to take seriously. Mr. Mann has added to the difficulties by displaying considerably more humor than is his usual solemn custom. And he has contrived two other obstacles to complete acceptance of his legend at its face value. The first is the style, an arch and peculiar mélange of pseudomedieval mannerisms, archaic and obsolete words, Latin and French phrases. Compared with it, the old-fashioned historical novels, whose pages were clotted with " 'Od's bloods" and "prithees," were works of simple realism.

The other technical device in *The Holy Sinner* that distracts and confounds is the dialogue. An exaggeration and near parody of the general style, it often teeters on the edge of the absurd and ludicrous. One feels that Mr. Mann has his tongue in his cheek and is rather ponderously amused by his own skill in arranging words so preposterously.

The Holy Sinner is a strange performance, a pastiche of labored humor, childish romance, Christian faith, spiritual allegory, outlandish mannerisms—all served up with dash and vigor and vast technical dexterity. Approached literally it can easily seem silly; read with imagination and the patience to ponder on its symbolism and possible interpretations it can as easily seem brilliant and profound.

Thomas Mann is a great writer. In his seventies he is even more intellectually formidable than he was thirty years ago. But *The Magic Mountain* remains his finest achievement. That, too, was a philosophical novel heavily burdened with abstract discussion. But *The Magic Mountain* presented its ideas through the minds of several fascinating and significantly representative characters; and told a story, too—a slow-moving one, but still a story. It made all the difference.

When William Faulkner received the Nobel Prize he made the only public speech of his life. It was a simple, modest and noble expression of a profound truth about art. Its crux consisted of these two paragraphs:

"Our tragedy today is a general and universal physical fear

so long sustained by now that we can even bear it. There are no longer problems of the spirit. There is only the question: when will I be blown up? Because of this, the young man or woman writing today has forgotten the problems of the human heart in conflict with itself which alone can make good writing because only that is worth writing about, worth the agony and the sweat.

"He must learn them again. He must teach himself that the basest of all things is to be afraid; and, teaching himself that, forget it forever, leaving no room in his workshop for anything but the old verities and truths of the heart, the old universal truths lacking which any story is ephemeral and doomed—love and honor and pity and pride and compassion and sacrifice. Until he does so, he labors under a curse. He writes not of love but of lust, of defeats in which nobody loses anything of value, of victories without hope and, worst of all, without pity or compassion. His griefs grieve on no universal bones, leaving no scars. He writes not of the heart but of the glands."

That the truths and problems of the human heart are the great subject of fiction should be axiomatic. That too often today novelists write only of the glands is sadly obvious. And, ironic though it may be, no modern novelist of rank has written more often of glandular conduct than William Faulkner. At the same time he has displayed a profound understanding of the heart and has consistently buried that understanding beneath a slag pile of turgid words.

William Faulkner was born in New Albany, Mississippi, in 1897. He had not finished high school when he enlisted in the Royal Canadian Air Force in the First World War. After the war he went to college for only one year. Since then he has spent most of his life in Oxford, Mississippi, hunting, fishing, farming and writing. "I'm just a writer. Not a literary man," he has said. "I write about the people around Oxford. I know them and they know me. They don't much care what I write." He has written two volumes of poetry, five collections of short stories and thirteen novels.

No modern writer has suffered more extravagant overpraise or more ignorant abuse than William Faulkner. In France, where he is the most admired of American writers, critics fervently hymn his "anguished style" and talk about "the tangible presence of God" in his works. In this country critical opinion is sharply divided, and his most widely read book is his most sensational, the gruesomely revolting *Sanctuary*.

William Faulkner, who is probably the most naturally gifted of contemporary American novelists, has never bothered to master the rudiments of his craft. Thomas Wolfe, who died young, knew that he had failed in the same way and tried desperately, although with small success, to make his later books less disorderly and inchoate than his first. Mr. Faulkner with perverse arrogance, or, as his more fanatical admirers claim, with the pride and lonely self-absorption of genius, challenges his readers to understand or be interested in his stories. But his dark, elliptic, violent books, unsuccessful as fiction as most of them are, yet contain such flashes of power, the impact of so sensitive a personality gone nearly berserk with fury, that they present a fascinating literary problem.

Most Faulkner novels and short stories deal with the life and history of an impossible never-never land of his imagination, Yoknapatawpha County, Mississippi. They present a grotesquely distorted, intricately complicated, nightmare vision of the South: its pioneer past, its plantation aristocracy, the heroic epic of the Civil War, the rise of the poor whites to business

[86]

importance, and the long, silent patience of the Negro. Mr. Faulkner yearns for the aristocratic codes of the lost plantation society, but never forgets that slavery was a curse that still lies dark on the land. He despises utterly the business ethics of the twentieth century and sees most of modern life as a sink of corruption. Most of his characters are obsessed by strange fears, ridden by lust, driven by private furies. Some of them are mighty men, larger than life; more of them are warped and evil, cruel and degenerate. A miasma of hate lies low over Yoknapatawpha County.

The dank and sinister world in which Mr. Faulkner dwells bears little resemblance to the actual Oxford in which he eats, sleeps and writes. It is really a mythological world, inhabited by symbolical characters, echoing with ponderous poetry. And poetry is the essence of Mr. Faulkner's creation. By verbal incantations he does create powerful and haunting emotions. The very density of his prolix, clumsy and agonized prose, which so often seems a triumph of useless obfuscation, can occasionally convey emotional atmosphere with magical effectiveness.

But if the famed Faulkner style is sometimes wonderful it is more often disastrous. Its peculiar words used peculiarly, its outrageous syntax, its breathless incoherence and marathon sentences confound confusion. Its sheer sloppiness is an affront to any standards of fictional technique. Yet Mr. Faulkner is obsessed with technique and experiments with it constantly: shifting narrators and points of view, flying mysteriously about in time and space, defying chronology and ignoring decent probabilities. Many of his characters talk the wildest kind of Faulknerese.

It is such literary crimes and misdemeanors which sabotage

the artistic success of Mr. Faulkner's novels. But it is their excessive emphasis on one kind of human behavior, the basest, that makes Mr. Faulkner's novels seem so out of proportion and so far from the realities of Southern life. Some of the world's greatest novels have been written about psychopaths and criminals. Mr. Faulkner has written about violence, murder and madness in nearly all of his, and about a variety of sexual abnormalities in many of them—rape, miscegenation, incest and revolting unnatural vice. Why, one wonders.

In view of all this it is proof of Mr. Faulkner's enormous talent that his work is as striking as it is. His books are marked by a cruel humor and flashes of penetrating insight. Embedded in them, far below the surface scum of tortured words, intensely dramatic stories often lie. Major problems of life and character are often glimpsed, if not illuminated. But Mr. Faulkner's characters themselves are nearly always savage symbols; they rarely have a life of their own as memorable individuals.

Some responsible critics have been unduly impressed by the fact that the Faulkner novels and short stories can be linked together as one panoramic, fictional history of Yoknapatawpha County. But this seems to me to be an entirely irrelevant factor. Any particular book is not better or more significant because its author has written others about the same locality. Books must stand on their own merits. Trollope's *Barchester Towers* is admired and beloved for its charm and wit and wisdom, not because it is the second book in a series about an English shire.

It is equally mistaken, it seems to me, to give an author high marks for effort and good intentions. It is the results which count. Mr. Faulkner's novels are interesting because of his great and undisciplined talent. But they are hamstrung by their faults. That Mr. Faulkner is a serious artist is to his credit; but it does not atone for his impenetrable prose.

There have been five Faulkner books since 1940, not counting a collection of his short stories and a selection of his work in the Portable Library. *The Hamlet,* which was published in the spring of 1940, is a novel about Mr. Faulkner's celebrated poor-white family, the Snopes. That malignant tribe of human vermin is portrayed on the rise to business and social eminence, a rise made possible by their guile, energy and lack of moral scruples. There is some gusty frontier humor in *The Hamlet* and more than the usual quota of cupidity, lust, arson, murder and sickening unnatural vice. The style, which sometimes seems to possess the paralyzing power of a boa constrictor, is frequently unintelligible.

The Hamlet is as pure and typically Faulknerian as any of his books, so gross an indulgence in his worst mannerisms that if someone else had written it it would be considered a cruel and brilliant parody.

Two years later came *Go Down Moses,* a collection of short stories about the members of one family through a hundred years, both decadent aristocrats and illegitimate colored relations. It is an important contribution to the Faulknerian demonology because it contains "The Bear," a long novelette which is a superb hunting story when it is clear (well, comparatively clear) and a pretentious nightmare when it relapses into some of the most atrocious verbiage Mr. Faulkner ever committed.

Mr. Faulkner's next novel, *Intruder in the Dust,* is one of his least ambitious efforts. It is the simple story of a courageous boy's success in preventing the lynching of an innocent Negro.

[89]

Its likable characters and lack of any sexual motivation make it seem uncharacteristic. But its many passages of conventionally tortuous prose keep it in the official canon. It is more pleasant and more lucid, but less striking and less powerful than its predecessors.

Little need be said of *Knight's Gambit,* a collection of five short stories and one novelette. The short stories are exceedingly minor efforts, and the novelette is not impressive. All concern some amateur detective work in Yoknapatawpha County and so add their bit to the total panorama.

The fifth Faulkner book of the last decade is *Requiem for a Nun,* one of his strangest. It is no longer surprising to find his prose as viscous as molasses in January. But to find two different books with no real connection whatever between them alternating in sections under one title still seems strange and purposeless —even though Mr. Faulkner did the same thing once before, in *The Wild Palms.* And it seems stranger still to discover that one of the books is a three-act play printed in dramatic form.

The first book in *Requiem for a Nun* consists of a recapitulation of the history of Yoknapatawpha County from early in the nineteenth century until 1951, a long and melancholy survey of the past in which all of Mr. Faulkner's usual themes and many of his famous characters are briefly mentioned.

The second book, the play, is a sequel to *Sanctuary,* Mr. Faulkner's most popular and most sensationally revolting novel. It takes up the story of Temple Drake and Gowan Stevens eight years later, but wastes much of its space recalling all the horrors of *Sanctuary.* The theme of the play is evil and repentance, and the points at issue are: Why did the colored nurse murder Temple's baby, and what was Temple's guilt in the matter, and has Temple any chance of purging herself of her sins?

[90]

The Eminently Obscure

Because the theme of guilt and repentance is a great one, it would be easy to overestimate this stilted, artificial and morbid little play. But, it seems to me, Mr. Faulkner has failed to handle his theme effectively. *Requiem for a Nun* is a flat and disappointing book. Neither of its disparate halves is an important addition to Mr. Faulkner's work.

William Faulkner shares his belief in the value of obscurity (an emotional value?) with many other modern writers, although his particular kind of assault on the English language is his own invention. The sexual crimes and "social degeneration" with which he is preoccupied are also recurring themes in much modern fiction. The hate, terror and spasms of pity which mark his work are like exaggerated and distorted reflections of the sorriest aspects of twentieth-century life.

It seems almost as if Mr. Faulkner, who is so uniquely himself and imitates no writer living or dead, is a typical modern writer after all. His refusal to write lucidly is a common expression of intellectual arrogance combined with literary sloppiness. The concentration on vice and violence, which is his morose comment on a declining civilization, is characteristic of many of his bitter and frightened contemporaries.

VI

COMRADES OF THE COTERIE:

Henry Green, Compton-Burnett, Bowen, Graham Greene

> "If this young man expresses himself
>   In terms too deep for *me,*
> Why, what a very singularly deep young man
>   This deep young man must be!"
> —*W. S. Gilbert*

The dinner party wasn't going well. Mrs. Sterling looked across the table at her husband with a pretty little frown of anxiety. Harry was in one of his moods. That third old-fashioned, which he never should have taken, hadn't cheered him up a bit. Now he was staring at Mrs. Mandible in a positively rude way. Oh dear, were literary people worth the social risk? Mrs. Mandible was so very literary. She belonged to three different book clubs, in addition to being the chairman of the book department of the Woman's Civic Club. What was that she was saying to Harry now?

"What do you think of Henry Green, Mr. Sterling?"

"I'm afraid I don't know him," said Harry. "What outfit's he with?"

"Of course you don't know him. Nobody does. He's that Pseudonymous English writer nobody knows, the one who has pictures taken of the back of his head."

"Why?" asked Harry. "Is there something special about the back of his head?"

"No, no. How could he stay anonymous if his face showed? And it's ever so much better publicity to be shy about publicity. Everybody knows that. Remember Greta Garbo? I've just finished his new novel."

"What's it called?"

"Nothing."

"You mean it hasn't got a title? A book without a name by an anonymous writer really would be something."

"No, its name is *Nothing*. Green always uses queer names, *Beginning, Concluding, Loving*—names like that."

"What's it about?"

"Well, it isn't really about anything, Mr. Sterling, just some people in London talking. Green is supposed to be ever so subtle and original and a marvelous stylist. Lots of critics think he's brilliant. The adjectives they use about him! You'd think he was Swift and Shelley and Virginia Woolf combined. But I don't. Would you like to know what it's like?"

If Harry hadn't caught his wife's frantic signal he would have said, "God, no!" What he did say was: "Yes, I ought to keep more up to date on these things."

Mrs. Mandible drew a deep breath and addressed herself to the entire dinner party. "Well, it just goes to show the kind of books some people get excited about. This one's about three couples in London, unmarried couples if you know what I mean. This John Pomfret is a widower and a really frightful snob in a kindly way. And he has a girl called Liz who keeps hinting that she wants to be married and John pretends not to notice because he is really in love all the time with an old flame of his youth called Jane Weatherby who is a widow and who is having an affair with a man called Dick. What makes it so complicated is that John's daughter Mary gets engaged to Jane's son Philip and they are all so worried about poor old Arthur's leg."

"Whose leg?" demanded Harry.

"Just a friend of theirs. He had to have the toes cut off, and then the foot at the ankle and then the whole leg. It killed him."

"What did his leg have to do with the other people?"

"Nothing. They just keep talking in little short scenes, silly, inconsequential, foolish talk. None of them ever says right out loud what he's thinking about. But that Jane! She's supposed to be very charming in an idiotic fashion. I think her charm is pretty close to lunacy. But she does have a sort of low cunning. She breaks up the children's engagement and her own affair and John's affair and traps John into marrying her for old times' sake. But he's such a bore. I do prefer my rich, sophisticated characters to be clever. If they're not, they're so dull!"

When Mrs. Mandible paused for breath Mrs. Sterling thought that she had better say something before Harry did. "Isn't there any point to it?" she asked.

"I suppose there must be," replied Mrs. Mandible. "Or I mean that Green probably thinks there is. He says that *Nothing* is a 'frivolous comedy of manners.' It's frivolous all right; but it doesn't seem comic to me. If he's making fun of rich Londoners who led fashionably immoral lives in Mayfair twenty-five years ago and can't stop trying to live the same Noel-Coward-early-Evelyn-Waugh way today—why, he doesn't do it well at all. He seems to think that Jane's stupidity about her idiot little girl is funny. Jane keeps calling her a saint or a martyr and the child is just crazy, or nearly. And he makes a little fun of Jane's son Philip because he longs so for a stuffy, respectable life all knotted up with family ties and instead he has Jane for a mother.

"Maybe some people will think that *Nothing* is fun. It's written almost as much in dialogue as the novels of Ivy Compton-Burnett, but it hasn't any of her malice or wit or fiendish skill in digging into people. It's almost as light and foolish as an Angela Thirkell novel, but it hasn't her charm and humor. I think it's vacuous and insipid."

"Well, for goodness sake!" exploded Harry. "Why do you bother to read such stuff?"

"Why, you have to," said Mrs. Mandible, "if you want to keep up with the best literature."

The reason Mrs. Mandible felt she had to read *Nothing* was because she read criticism (and took it seriously) as well as books. She read reviews in daily and Sunday newspapers, in weekly and monthly magazines, and in academic quarterlies. She was often bewildered by the diversity of critical opinion and she was not perceptive enough to distinguish which reviewers were admiring what books and for what reasons. If a number of critical voices were joined in applause, that was enough for her. Naturally, then, it was inevitable that she would frequently be lured into reading the clever but anemic and pretentious works of the coterie writers.

A coterie writer is usually blessed with genuine talents; but he uses them to write peculiar, artificially mannered novels of strictly limited appeal which are extravagantly overpraised by the few critics whose pride it is to admire books which lesser mortals don't appreciate. This kind of thing, of course, has been going on at least since the invention of movable type. The reefs of literature are strewn with the wrecks of deflated

[95]

reputations, the reputations of authors who once knew a brief hour of transient glory. Some critic intent on displaying his own unusual discrimination "discovered" them. Others scrambled on the band wagon, pretending that they had been aware of So-and-so's unique importance all the time. If So-and-so's books were written in a Mandarin style of painful artificiality, if they were symbolical or ambiguous or opaque, if they required a major feat of self-hypnosis on their reader's part for appreciation of their trivial merits, so much the better.

A characteristic example of a coterie writer is James Branch Cabell, a minor writer of lacquered fantasies whose overvaluation in the 1920s was something fantastic. Mr. Cabell was a graceful stylist; but his sniggering sort of wit appealed principally to adolescents proud of the fact that they were "sophisticated" enough to recognize Mr. Cabell's far from subtle indelicacies.

Ronald Firbank, the English chronicler of lunatic degeneracy, is another example of the kind of minor talent dear to the coteries.

But if many modern coterie writers are sadly preoccupied with sexual degeneracy (we will take up some current exemplars of this in the following chapter), others are worth much more serious consideration. Their books are free of mincing affectations, there is method in the madness of their verbal acrobatics. They are coterie books because they are experiments in technique and subject matter, experiments which are not completely successful and which repel the interest of the average cultivated reader (mythical creature!). When a writer of near genius, a James Joyce or a William Faulkner, writes such a book he can transcend the limitations of coterie writing. When less blazingly gifted mortals try their hand at it the results are less likely to be rewarding. Students of the craft of fiction, and congenial spirits who share the author's enthusiasm for whatever blind alley he chooses to explore, are the only two groups who will feel that they have not wasted time and money in the curious company of the coterie.

During the last decade most of the able and interesting experimenters who won the favor of critically fashionable coteries were English; and most of the dabblers in degeneracy who won coterie applause were American.

The Henry Green who so confounded Mrs. Mandible is an English manufacturer who writes books in his spare time, an hour each evening. So far six of his novels have been published in this country, *Loving, Nothing, Back, Concluding, Caught* and *Party Going.* They all bear the stamp of Mr. Green's peculiar literary personality; they all display unmistakable evidence of Mr. Green's wit, his remarkable ear for the fatuous monotony of everyday speech, and his complete indifference to conventional methods of narration and characterization. Designed to shed obliquely satirical comments on various aspects of English life, they manage to demonstrate Mr. Green's cleverness without seeming sufficiently clever themselves to reward the effort of reading them. *Back* is a good example of the prevailingly arid climate of his work.

This is a novel about a soldier home from the wars, minus a leg, suffering from profound psychological shock. Charley was shy, bumbling, subject to mental blanks. His difficulties in readjusting himself to civilian life were immensely complicated by his involvement in a case of mistaken identity. Charley mistook a woman he had never previously known for the dead woman he had formerly loved. A story of a man more deeply wounded in his mind than in his body, pitifully searching for

[97]

the woman who had meant love and peace and happiness before the war, could be moving and psychologically interesting. But *Back* is neither.

Charley is too vague and simple-minded to have any depth or much reality. If *Back* were really successful, Charley would secure a firm grip on the reader's sympathies. But he does nothing of the kind. Charley is as shadowy as the friend of a friend in a snapshot taken by an inexpert photographer on a cloudy day. He is only a symbol of all wounded, bewildered veterans, the most important symbol in a book crowded with them. His girl, Rose, is one, too; and so are the word "rose" and the quality of rosiness. There isn't much rosiness in the postwar world for the Charleys.

The dialogue in *Back* is so accurate, so faithful to the inability of many ordinary people to express themselves effectively, that it is eloquently dull. No one of its characters ever says a thing worth hearing, ever opens his mouth without wallowing in bromides and clichés, without spouting hackneyed banalities. Such talk is real enough; but it is marvelously tedious. Colloquial speech ought to make characters seem vital and real. But somehow in *Back* it remains mere words, phonographically correct no doubt, but the words of surface types, not of interesting individuals.

Back is a story about a potentially poignant and dramatic situation written in such a dry and fussy way that all the poignance and drama have been squeezed out of it. Henry Green is clever and moderately gifted. But his novels are thin and pulpy and lack literary nourishment.

A sharper wit, a more original form and the presence of a more striking personality distinguish the remarkable novels of Ivy Compton-Burnett. Peculiar, difficult, artificial as the periwigs of Louis XIV, these coldly witty and cruelly malicious satires are intimidatingly brilliant. Even when they are as dull and tiresome as her last one, *Darkness and Day,* they still are impressive in a gruesome way. When they are as witheringly comic as *Bullivant and the Lambs,* or even as devastating as the less triumphant *Two Worlds and Their Ways,* they are almost overpowering. I can't pretend to like them, or to enjoy them; but it is nearly impossible not to feel in their presence the uneasy respect and instinctive alarm of a rabbit staring from a safe distance at a boa constrictor.

All of Ivy Compton-Burnett's novels are satires of the least attractive aspects of human nature as found among the nobility and landed gentry in the 1890s or thereabouts. All of them are written almost exclusively in dialogue, with only an occasional stage direction to set a scene or get characters from one room to another. Sometimes even these minimum aids to understanding are dispensed with. People speak up without having been introduced and without previous acknowledgment of their presence. It is puzzling at first; but a puzzle which requires only some conscientious application for its solution.

What is more startling is the dialogue itself. All the characters in an Ivy Compton-Burnett novel—masters, servants and children alike—talk with the polysyllabic majesty of Samuel Johnson, with the passion for precise meanings of Henry James (but not with his complexity of syntax) and with the uninhibited enthusiasm for self-expression of the thoroughly conditioned products of an ultraprogressive education. Heroic couplets or blank verse would be realistic compared with this fabulous talk, which consists of self-revelation, self-analysis, epigram, paradox, conversational lunge, parry and riposte, caustic and malicious sarcasm and cryptic innuendo. Brutally frank and nakedly uninhibited, wise with the brittle wisdom of cynicism and the weary wisdom of suffering, it makes for exhausting reading.

Although everybody talks in the same way, with the same incredible command of words, the characters do speak for themselves. The demon children don't say the same things as the glacial butlers or the cynical old men. But nearly everything said contributes to Miss Compton-Burnett's ruthless and feline satire of the commonest of human sins—selfishness, cruelty and hypocrisy. No writer of our time has a more despairingly low opinion of his fellow creatures than she has. And yet, deep beneath the cold glitter of her books, one can occasionally perceive traces of sincere compassion for unhappy mortals.

Another element which adds to the weird sense of unreality in these strange novels is their grotesquely melodramatic plots. Perhaps Miss Compton-Burnett feels that she must do something to make up for the torrential loquaciousness of her characters. What she does is to involve them in complex intrigues centered about problems of wills, heirs, missing papers, incest, theft, etc. These old-fashioned plots, however, are too unreal and ridiculous to add any narrative suspense to Miss Compton-Burnett's stories, which must stand or fall on their merits as tours de force of satirical dialogue.

It is no wonder, then, that such highly seasoned and exotic dishes remain caviar to the general. And even those who can appreciate them find that a little goes an exceedingly long way. Miss Compton-Burnett strikes her one note with bravura skill and awe-inspiring aplomb; but she always strikes the same note, and that grows tiresome. So she, too, writes not for a general audience, but for the small coterie which, after the manner of coteries, extravagantly overvalues her incontestable brilliance.

Probably the most authentic talent for the creative function of fiction among the English writers grouped together here under the banner of the coterie is that of the sensitive, fastidious and astute Anglo-Irish woman, Elizabeth Bowen. Mrs. Bowen is a novelist, a short-story writer and an essayist—and a book reviewer whose inordinate generosity toward mediocre novels by her compatriots always seems wildly out of character. Several of her best works, such novels as *To the North* and *The Death of the Heart,* appeared in the 1930s. In the last decade she has been represented by a book about her ancestral home in Ireland, a book about an Irish hotel, two volumes of short stories and a novel, *The Heat of the Day*. It is this last book in particular which establishes her claim for inclusion in the present chapter.

As a short-story writer, Mrs. Bowen has followed the examples of Chekhov and Katherine Mansfield, concentrating on creation of a mood, insight into character and emotional atmosphere. Only occasionally has she bothered with neatly constructed plots, but when she has, she has handled them expertly. She is fond of indirection and implication and is proficient in the oblique approach. The stories in *Look at All Those Roses* and *Ivy Gripped the Steps* are often thin and intellectually subtle to the point of elusiveness; but they are distinguished work.

With precise and cool dexterity, in a limpid and lovely style which avoids every obvious trick used by others to gain dramatic force and emotional impact, they explore refinements of feeling and sensation, intangibles of emotion and atmosphere. The lucidity of Mrs. Bowen's prose is deceptive, for the themes of her stories are usually just suggested, are never diagramed and driven home with dramatic action and exciting climaxes. Since she deals with emotional tempests in a purely intellectual fashion, she seems formally aloof at first; but soon one perceives beneath her ultra drawing-room manner a warm compassion, an almost intuitive sensitivity which can shed a sudden and unexpected light on the heartaches and submerged anguish of living.

Subtle, patrician, frankly literary, Mrs. Bowen's short stories challenge the imagination of perceptive readers. The secret places of the wounded heart and the emotional conflicts of the sheltered life are illuminated in brilliant flashes, with insight and with charm—but the pastel shades and delicate draftsmanship of her work hold little appeal for readers accustomed to the gaudier colors and broader, heavier lines of most popular fiction.

When Mrs. Bowen wrote *The Heat of the Day* and came to consider a more concrete theme than is her usual custom, a theme directly connected with the Second World War, she paradoxically seemed to retreat farther than ever before into the cool privacy of her own mind. Her novel dealt with the psychological pressures of war and a melodramatic possibility of treason; but somehow it turned out to be the most abstract and purely personal book Mrs. Bowen has yet written.

There are many penetrating passages, illuminating ideas and suggestive implications in *The Heat of the Day*. They command and deserve admiration. Mrs. Bowen never wrote a shoddy or commonplace page in her life. But *The Heat of the Day* fails in the essential illusion of fiction. Its principal characters are spectral wraiths haunting the dim corridors of their creator's mind, never believable human beings.

Comrades of the Coterie

This curiously abstract novel about people existing in a void concerns an acute emotional crisis—but communicates no feeling at all. It is about people involved in a dramatic conflict—but it is so filled with hairsplitting introspection and speculative reveries that it seems pale and drained of all vitality. Its characters think unnaturally "literary" thoughts. They indulge in what one of them herself calls "impossible conversations." The prose in which their story is told is intricate and exquisitely wrought; but it is opaque, obscure and soft. There is nothing to grasp firmly in *The Heat of the Day,* no inner core, only the lights and shades, the delicate sensibility and the analytical niceties of Mrs. Bowen's own mind. And these are incongruous bedfellows for a story about love, emotional blackmail and espionage.

The Heat of the Day is a triangle story about Stella, an attractive widow of forty; Robert, her lover; and Harrison, a mysterious stranger in the counterespionage service, who offers to refrain from arresting Robert as a spy if he can replace him in Stella's affections. Such a situation cries out for the sure hand of an expert in psychological thrillers. Mrs. Bowen, who shuns the explicit like cholera and refuses to supply explanatory motivations, circles all around the central problem of her story without ever explaining it.

Her characters are not only unreal; they act parts for which they seem perversely miscast. They speak lines which make little sense. And Mrs. Bowen says things about them which make even less: "She was at a desirable distance from her soul." Such an idea may mean something to Mrs. Bowen, but to more earth-bound minds it is unintelligible. There are good things in *The Heat of the Day,* vivid impressions of wartime London and brilliant silhouettes of minor characters. But its total effect is negative; it arouses neither belief nor interest.

Elizabeth Bowen is a brilliant woman who knows much about human character and much about the craft of fiction. Why, then, did she choose to write a novel like this? The question haunts the mind. She has written indirectly before. But never before has she deliberately parodied reality, deliberately killed the vital core of her book so that only a few sprigs of wit and observation curl around its edges. Can she have come to believe that a subtle, abstract thought is worth a petrified character? An exquisitely rendered fleeting sensation worth a reaction of persistent incredulity? Has the character-creating, storytelling function of fiction come to bore her?

These sadly pertinent questions must remain unanswered. But the fact that they arise at all is demonstration enough that Mrs. Bowen has chosen to enlist among the coterie writers and devote her fine talents to decorating the outer fringes of fiction, leaving the all-important center mysteriously empty. Since her own mind is interesting, her style impeccable and her fringe-work expert, there will always be a limited number of readers who will value her writing highly and forgive the basic failure of a book like *The Heat of the Day*.

The three novelists we have been discussing, Henry Green, Ivy Compton-Burnett and Elizabeth Bowen, all belong in the coterie classification because of their somewhat similar reaction to the modern world. Disliking it intensely, finding it a cruel chaos inhabited by unfortunate victims of forces too strong for them—the spiteful, stupid and unhappy—they retreat from direct communication with their contemporaries and write peculiar puzzles for their own amusement. Their creative gifts are real; but they find it more attractive to experiment with technique, to string together pearls of sensibility, rather than to interpret the main stream of life.

Comrades of the Coterie

A novel, I believe, should be built around a structural framework, with the intention of imposing a conscious design on a selection from experience. The novelist must be aware of the technique of his craft—just as an artist must have some unifying concept or design in his imagination in order to paint an effective picture. But excessive concentration on method rather than on matter is highly dangerous. It can reflect a feverish revolt against traditional cultural forms, an effete and unhealthy reaction which seems not far from decadence. When technique ceases to be a means and becomes an end in itself something is wrong, either in the artist or in his society.

It is, of course, a matter of opinion whether our three English novelists actually sin in this fashion. Their more fervent admirers do not think that they do. And it is obviously impossible to say where significant advances in technique leave off and sterile doodling begins. The novel is a superbly flexible artistic instrument, the finest device yet discovered by man wherewith to dramatize and interpret the infinitely rich and infinitely various experience of living. It is not subject to any laws made by individual critics, and it should not be. The justification of any particular method, mannerism or technique is acceptance by readers and imitation by other writers.

The experiments of James Joyce with the stream-of-consciousness technique were grotesque as well as brilliant; but they were extraordinarily fruitful. A judicious and restrained use of the stream-of-consciousness device will remain one of the novelist's most useful tools. Whether the weird dialogue of Miss Compton-Burnett or the palely loitering specters of Mrs. Bowen's latest novel are experiments noble in purpose or examples of a sort of modern literary decadence is a legitimate question for debate. I am inclined myself to suspect the worst.

In My Opinion

Although Graham Greene dislikes the century in which he is condemned to live as intensely as his compatriots whom we have just discussed, his reaction to it is somewhat different. Like them he has retreated in some of his work from the crass pleasures of direct communication to the more rarefied delights of indirection and ambiguity; but his entire outlook is molded by the fact that he is a devout convert to the Roman Catholic Church.

For Graham Greene this has meant that his already cryptic work has been complicated by points of Catholic doctrine beyond the understanding of Protestant or unbelieving readers. His best-known book, *The Heart of the Matter,* hinges on a concept of grace which Mr. Greene does not explain to the ignorant. The result is a protagonist whose motivation seems bewilderingly mysterious; but it may not be for those who carry the right key. In any case, it produced an anomalous situation where *The Heart of the Matter* was overpraised by critics and readers who did not understand what it was really about, and where many readers who admired Mr. Greene's technical facility were baffled by his theme. He is probably not in intention a deliberate coterie recruit, but in effect he has at least an associate membership.

Graham Greene is cultivated, highly educated, widely traveled and sophisticated, as well as devout. Much of his work has been savagely sarcastic, some of it morosely misanthropic. His novels usually explore sinister psychological depths, particularly neuroses caused by fear and guilt. They are divided into two groups: murder and espionage thrillers, and more serious efforts concerned with religious and theological themes. The first group is considerably the more successful. But it is the second, *The Heart of the Matter* variety, which has made him famous.

[106]

Comrades of the Coterie

The Ministry of Fear (superb title!), which was published in 1943, is Mr. Greene's latest thriller. It is a good example of his skill in achieving certain limited effects. Mr. Greene is a master of the sinister suggestion and the unexpected understatement; but he nearly always destroys the suspense and emotional impact of his stories by a vague allusiveness, a clutter of irrelevant material, unsatisfactory motivations and disappointing denouements. Sometimes he even overwrites. As a spy story and a psychological melodrama exploring the emotions of pity and fear, *The Ministry of Fear* gets off to an excellent start, builds up some engrossing complications and then peters out sadly. And its climax, a gory massacre, ends all its problems without solving or adequately explaining them.

There are quite bloodcurdling situations in *The Ministry of Fear* and some grand background of London during the blitz. But Mr. Greene's broodings on "the horrible and horrifying emotion of pity . . . the sense of pity which is so much more promiscuous than lust" are suggestively sinister rather than an understandable and integral part of his story. They don't succeed in raising *The Ministry of Fear* above the level of a de luxe spy story, although that seems to be their purpose.

Pity is the crucial emotion also in *The Heart of the Matter,* which is a fictional study of an essentially good man, a devout Roman Catholic, whose kindness and pity for others involve him in actions forbidden by his religion. Mr. Greene has handled his minor characters expertly and his exotic West African background extremely well. But he has not been successful in his major theme. He inspires doubt in his readers' minds, rather than either pity or admiration for his perplexed hero.

If his hero really believed that he was damning his soul for eternity would he have done what he did for the sake of the

[107]

temporary, earthly happiness of two neurotic women—merely to spare their feelings? Is pity a strong enough motive for such a sacrifice? Was the hero actually a heretic who believed it better to lose his soul than to hurt others? It is here that fine points of Catholic doctrine, of grace and salvation, enter. Perhaps they make everything understandable; but they can do so for readers only with the necessary theological preparation. Successful fiction, I believe, must not be a matter for the initiated only. An inner conflict based on a point of religious doctrine could be a moving and psychologically important and interesting theme for a novel, but only if the point at issue is explained, in words of one syllable if necessary, for readers of other faiths.

Graham Greene's latest novel, *The End of the Affair,* is also a profoundly Catholic novel, and a considerably less successful one. It is the story of the birth and growth of saintly religious faith in a most unlikely individual, a shallow and promiscuous woman deeply involved in an adulterous love affair. Written in the first person by the heroine's self-centered, cynical and malicious lover, this reverent story of the love of God and God's love fails utterly to be convincing.

Mr. Greene displays his usual distinctive flair for words and atmosphere. His precise, carved sentences fit together like stone blocks which require no mortar. But his author's hands jerking his puppet strings are always noticeable. He is not content to demonstrate his thesis with one religious conversion. He adds two more, both of them even more unlikely. He even makes use of several near miracles. It is too much. *The End of the Affair* is not only unconvincing; it is dull.

That this is a carefully written novel is obvious. That it is a desperately earnest one is also. But its only value is as a religious tract. Graham Greene can do wonderful things with the English language; but verbal skill alone cannot make up for inadequate characterization and unconvincing motivation. Nor can an atmosphere of sardonic disillusionment make a modern miracle convincing.

Graham Greene is a writer of short stories as well as of novels. In *Nineteen Stories* examples of his work originally written between 1929 and 1948 were published in book form. Slight, bleak and dismal they were, too, most of them disappointing and strangely flat. They deal with Mr. Greene's favorite themes, fear, futility, cheap nastiness, grotesque horror, spiritual poverty and theology. It is a repellent world which Mr. Greene inhabits in these tales, a world where children cower in terror, where weaklings crawl through miserable lives, where shabby crooks practice cheap frauds and petty rackets. Vulgarity oozes everywhere and issues of good and evil are so rarely faced that evil flourishes like the green bay tree.

Fear is normal in Mr. Greene's world and naturally to be expected; and lack of courage to meet it is nearly as normal. Mr. Greene forgives the cowardice of the child in his best story, "The Basement Room," but he cannot find it in him to forgive the cowardly adult in "A Drive in the County." Four or five of these stories are written with such cold skill that they are highly effective. The rest are mediocre.

Looking at the modern world around him with a mixture of fascination and repulsion, Mr. Greene found men and women "doing things in the dark which frightened them." And turning to the grimmer teachings of his Church he reminds himself and his readers that "when one is dead there's no unconsciousness any more forever."

VII

THE YOUNG DECADENTS:

Capote, Bowles, Buechner, Goyen, Williams, Yorke

"If he does really think that there is no distinction between virtue and vice, why, sir, when he leaves our houses let us count our spoons."—*Samuel Johnson*

There is no subject about which people think with more prejudice and more jangled emotions than the excesses of sex. We may live in an age of pseudotolerance and aggressive freedom to speak about matters formerly unspeakable, but few of us are qualified to do so with even a modicum of objectivity. We cannot escape the attitudes prevalent in our social circles when young. A man of seventy-five and a boy of twenty, like parallel lines, can never find an intellectual meeting place on this popular subject—no matter how far they extend their discussion.

Amateur exploration in the works of Freud and *The Kinsey Report* is not necessarily the beginnings of wisdom. It may provide the foundation for a deliberate effort to attain the humility not to judge and condemn, to escape the moral smugness which too often passes for virtue. But the conviction that sexual conduct is not always subject to rational choice and conscious control, and the recognition of the power of our glands and our personality as conditioned in childhood do not necessarily qualify us to write about sexual aberrations. And they certainly do not establish the worth of sexual extremes as a theme for fiction.

At this stage in the history of Western thought the entire subject of sexual extremes is so confused that rewarding treatment of it in fictional terms is extraordinarily difficult. It is still deeply enmeshed in the taboos of traditional morality, so deeply that reactions are usually either shocked protest or rebellious glee. And it is still too much the exclusive concern of the disciples of the wise man of Vienna for most novelists who write about it to do so with enough authority to be persuasive.

Whether particular sexual practices are right, wrong or neutral is not a matter on which modern men can agree. But that some practices are degenerate, abnormal and degrading is still the deep conviction of most members of our bewildered society. They feel that there is a distinction between natural sexuality and the departures from it which destroy or isolate some men and women. And the departures, they believe, should be regarded as clinical problems (to be understood with pity) or as vice. Can they be written about in fiction without the grave danger of idealizing psychopathic manifestations or vice (and such idealization is certainly decadent in itself), or the danger of amateur ax-grinding in the only partly explored domain of psychiatry?

The exceptions who avoid these dangers are few and writers of genius. Dostoevski could write magnificently about a whole catalogue of mental illness; Proust stressed the theme of homosexuality in his great novel. But only writers of such caliber can do so. And even Proust missed seeming a champion of degeneracy, rather than an historian of it, by only an eyelash. Nevertheless, a number of modern writers, most of them young, are

[111]

irresistibly attracted by sexual aberrations as subject matter for their novels. Many of them are definitely gifted, clever, unusually apt as stylists, sincerely devoted to the art of literary expression. But their preoccupation with nymphomania and homosexuality seems to me evidence of a decadent school in modern writing.

It would be easy to cite at least a dozen American novelists who have concentrated on some aspect of sexual degeneracy. Why they chose to do so is not clear. They usually do not write serious psychological studies which try to demonstrate the whys and wherefores. None of them seems to feel any disapproval from a moral point of view, or even the satirical distaste of a social critic. Such a viewpoint is not new among writers, but it is more prevalent today than ever before. A number of modern novelists write about matters which have always existed, with a sympathetic understanding close to apology so that some of their books seem travesties of responsible thinking, near glorifications of practices which should be regarded with all possible understanding, but which certainly should not be romanticized.

One possible motive, perhaps in some instances an unconscious one but not in all, is deliberate search for a new subject sensational enough to excite talk and controversy and so to stimulate sales. Another is the ultimate in individual, artistic rebellion against convention. To *épater les bourgeois* today it is no longer enough to sentimentalize prostitution or to glamourize promiscuity. Something more horrendous—that's the stuff to give the troops!

Some thoughtful critics have suggested that our modern decadents are only reflecting the moral anarchy of our time, a time in which there are no moral values at all. It is certainly true that there are no moral absolutes universally acknowledged today.

The Young Decadents

We do not all profess one faith and one church. Many of those who are nominally communicants of some religious denomination do not take its official dogmas seriously in their daily lives. Many people no longer put their trust in a fixed code of conduct, being too acutely aware of relative values, special circumstances and individual freedom.

But to admit all this is not the same as to agree that there are no values at all. Many people still cling to religious values; others strive to live by standards of honor and ethical conduct, others still by those of social responsibility. If we no longer believe that John Calvin or Jonathan Edwards had all the answers to problems of personal conduct we at least do not believe in moral anarchy. That way disintegration lies. The writers who deny the existence of any values at all and lament their own sophomoric despair are not only indulging in a sort of maudlin self-pity; they are degrading their stature as human beings.

When civilization shakes in the high wind of a political, economic and spiritual crisis, when the old order changeth and no man can foresee the new, then more than ever is the time for courage and decency, for faith in the values which give men dignity and make them worthy of respect. If we doubt the eternal flames of Hell because we think that Hell is here on earth right now, that is all the more reason why we should try to make the earth less like Hell by maintaining moral standards. Of course we should not throw stones. But if we wish to keep our society from going the way of Babylon and Rome we shouldn't throw bouquets either.

Several of the talented young writers who have chosen the darker corners of sex for literary themes possess enviable abilities. They are masters of mood and atmosphere, adroit arrangers of words into intricate and beautiful patterns, masters of fashionably abstruse symbolism. But even with these assets (although I don't really consider abstruseness an asset) they have a way of becoming so absorbed in technique itself and in their unhealthy themes that they neglect the development of interesting and significant characters. Prominent among them are Truman Capote and Paul Bowles.

Truman Capote has written some exotic and erotic short stories and a collection of slight travel sketches, but his small claim to fame rests on two novels, *Other Voices, Other Rooms,* which was published in 1948 when Mr. Capote was only twenty-three, and *The Grass Harp.* Unquestionably the work of an extraordinarily precocious and effective stylist, *Other Voices, Other Rooms* is a strange, opaque, sinister and sickening study of the crisis in a boy's life which sees him take the fork in the road that leads to homosexuality. Much of it is oblique and indirect so that the basic theme is clear enough, but the elaborate symbolism with which it is developed is not.

The appearance of a writer as young as Mr. Capote so fascinated by decadence that his whole book reeks with it, and so obsessed by the powers of evil, is a disturbing phenomenon. The recognizably real world known to most of us is not Mr. Capote's. Reality for him is not material and specific; it is emotional, poetic, symbolical, filled with sibilant whisperings and enigmatic verbal mysteries.

So it is not always possible to be certain of the meaning of his eloquent and reverberating prose. But it is impossible not to be impressed by the potent incantation he weaves in words. The bizarre atmosphere he conjures up is taut with suggestive implications. Crawling with luxuriant funguslike life, his pages are still and ominous, flickering with unholy light like the last five minutes before a summer cloudburst.

This kind of writing is spectacular, but it has little to do with a good novel. It is all mood and sound and fury, like Poe's hollow poem, "Ulalume." The characters are mere grotesques revealed in a glare which illuminates mannerisms and peculiarities and symbolical postures only, without conveying any depth or substance. They never seem real and the only conclusion reached is the depressing doom of the boy hero. The whole book seems like a trick, an illusion done with mirrors.

Other Voices, Other Rooms is the story of one summer in the life of its hero. Events are seen through the vague mind and constant hallucinations of its central character. The Deep South scene is a nightmare phantasmagoria, an appropriate background for this evil dream of defeat and degeneration. Although Mr. Capote fails to make his miserable boy's story seem either pitiful or significant, it is not for lack of sympathetic understanding. This, he seems to say, is an encounter with destiny, a very special kind of destiny. To lavish so much verbal splendor on such a theme seems to me trivial and perverse.

Compared with *Other Voices, Other Rooms, The Grass Harp* is sunny, cheerful and almost innocent. This fanciful novel about three eccentrics who rebel against an invasion of their private world by seeking refuge in a new one, a tree house in the woods by a cemetery, is a surprising item to come from Mr. Capote. Its prose is precise and cool and beautiful—and not at all baroque and overly ornate. It may be interpreted symbolically, but its symbolism is optional and simple, a far cry from the intricate obscurity of *Other Voices, Other Rooms.* Although it has a few lapses, it is a predominantly healthy and even an attractive little book.

It is attractive because of the new qualities Mr. Capote has

[115]

put into it—humor, fantasy, pathos. Truman Capote is so original a stylist, his macabre imagination is so peculiarly his own,
that everything he writes reflects his unique personality. But
The Grass Harp reflects a saner, better balanced aspect of his
personality than one would have suspected existed after reading
Other Voices, Other Rooms.

In his *The Sheltering Sky* Paul Bowles achieved a critical success similar to Mr. Capote's with *Other Voices, Other Rooms.*
His novel is not concerned with homosexuality, but it is about
spiritual degeneration, madness and self-destruction through
sexual depravity. And, like *Other Voices, Other Rooms,* although it is not written so ornately, it is brilliant in its evocation
of atmosphere and inadequate in its characterization. Some of
its episodes of sexual violence are brutally shocking, but they
are pointless. Others are the inevitable end of the train of events
Mr. Bowles set in motion.

This is a story of the North African desert and of the spiritual
desert in the souls of three Americans traveling there. Fleeing
from responsibility, from reality, from any positive relationships
with life, they find in the Sahara reflections of themselves. And
so they move through increasing decadence to ultimate disaster.
Uprooted, self-centered, egoistic, without beliefs or even interests, they lead a pointless, dreary and melancholy existence
traveling ever deeper into the desert and ever farther downward
into disloyalty, dishonesty, vice and degradation.

That Mr. Bowles means his noisome trio to symbolize many
others lost in the modern wasteland without faith, courage or
a minimum of decency and intelligence I have no doubt. But
his attitude toward his contemptible characters seems to me to
be equivocal. Instead of lashing out in rage, or in healthy satire,
he just looks at them sadly. There is no suggestion in his book

that these are three of the world's weaklings and parasites, people who have betrayed themselves and their society. On the contrary, the implication is that they are the natural consequence of the age in which they live, the age without values which we discussed a few pages earlier.

But people are not slaves of an intellectual fashion. They help shape a society as well as receive shape from it. Individuals cannot reverse the course of history; but they can cling to pride and courage and loyalty; they can stand at their posts like the Roman sentry dead but erect in the lava of Pompeii. If Mr. Bowles had delved into the psychological factors which formed his characters he might have had something interesting to say. It is his acceptance of their flabby souls as natural in the circumstances of modern life which offends.

Perhaps in the word acceptance we have the key to the whole decadent school of writing, acceptance or welcome of decay. Didactic moralizing is usually death to artistic fiction. But "no man is an island unto himself." No writer can escape expressing his own position on the nature, rights and duties of man. The position taken by the decadent writers is one of abject surrender.

An interesting phenomenon common to many of our modern decadent writers is their preoccupation with florid arabesques of style and intricate symbolism. It seems almost as if the less they have to say the more intent they are on saying it ornately. The weaker and more degenerate their characters the more elaborate their technique! A typical example of this is Frederick Buechner, whose *A Long Day's Dying* appeared in 1950 when he, too, was only twenty-three. Mr. Buechner strangled his dull and nasty story in festoons of rhetoric and smothered it beneath mountains of abstruse symbolism. His prose is a pale and synthetic imitation of the elderly Henry James at his most abstract and parenthetical. His symbolism is all tied up with the Greek legend of Tereus and Philomela, but in such an indirect fashion that it only adds confusion to the already opaque story. In his effort to be fashionable according to the shibboleths of a few literary Alexandrians Mr. Buechner killed the little chance he had of making his novel interesting or significant.

A Long Day's Dying is a study of the exquisite sensibilities and distraught emotions of several spineless and ineffectual people whose only purpose in life is to indulge their appetites and to wallow in self-pity. They are intellectual and moral pygmies. Mr. Buechner neither understood nor condemned them. He just used them as the pegs on which to hang his experiment in literary technique. It was all the more depressing because Mr. Buechner is obviously talented, obviously sincerely interested in the art of literary expression.

Similar in its pretentiousness, in its preoccupation with weak and degenerate characters defeated by life, in its turgid and fancy prose, is *The House of Breath* by William Goyen. This unbelievably stilted prose poem lamenting the decay and erosion of a Southern family is marked by passages of real narrative power; but most of it is close to absurdity. Some of its raptures are almost meaningless. Dripping with undigested emotion, incoherent and maudlin, infected with the homosexual theme so dear to many of the modern decadent writers, *The House of Breath* is a pitiful example of misdirected and squandered talents.

Two more examples of our current plague of literary decadence should be enough to demonstrate its nature and provide evidence of its prevalence. They are *The Roman Spring of Mrs. Stone* by Tennessee Williams and *The Widow* by Susan Yorke. Both are about rich and corrupt widows obsessed by men much

younger than themselves. But the evil in Mr. Williams' widow
is weak, leading to her progressive degeneration. The evil in
Miss Yorke's widow is strong, leading to her destruction of another. A nastier pair would be hard to come by in a year's safari
through the dampest and most dismal swamps of modern fiction.

Tennessee Williams is the celebrated young playwright who
wrote *The Glass Menagerie* and *A Streetcar Named Desire,*
those theatrical smashes about the unhappiness of psychopathic
Southern ladies. Those plays were unpleasant, but wonderfully
powerful and compassionate. *The Roman Spring of Mrs. Stone,*
his first novel, has none of their power or their pity. It is only
an erotic and depressing study of the mental and moral disintegration of a shallow and brittle character. It is drenched from
beginning to end in several kinds of sexual depravity.

The heroine of *The Roman Spring of Mrs. Stone* is a middle-
aged actress who sinks to the ultimate depths because of vanity
and loneliness, rather than for love or even lust. She is not a
significant, a well-portrayed or even an interesting character.
Her story is superficial, offensive and dull. Why a writer of
Mr. Williams' ability should have bothered with so trivial a
treatment of such a theme is difficult to imagine. Since he has
nothing of interest to say about it, the only point of view which
can be found in his pages is his own enthusiasm for his subject.

Miss Yorke's *The Widow,* while it is equally gruesome, is at
least successful as a melodramatic story. It is a study of a truly
vicious woman. It is also a "stunt" novel written in the form of
a memoir addressed by a woman to her dead lover. The widow
tells her lover many things he knew while he was still alive and
many things he didn't, things which would have curdled his
blood had he known them. No names are used. The widow is

"I" and the lover "you." Whether such technical devices are an asset is doubtful. In any case, this is an appalling psychological melodrama about a she-devil, who, it seems to me, is suffering the first symptoms of madness.

The widow is rich, beautiful, fashionable, clever, sophisticated, cultivated and egoistic. She is also selfish, sensual and corrupt. She falls in love with a weak young roué. She sees his faults with cold clarity. But she loves him in her fashion.

Her fashion is inspired by her conviction that love is a duel for power. Her lover is her enemy whom she seeks first to dominate and then to destroy. That love could be idealistic, compounded of affection, loyalty, tenderness and self-sacrifice, would seem to her mere mawkish sentimentality. The widow is so bottomlessly, so cruelly cynical that she never seems quite real. Mad she probably is. A lurid villainess she certainly is. A contemptible degenerate she certainly is, too.

Miss Yorke is a clever writer and has written her book cleverly. It is undeniably arresting. But it is a showy, bravura performance, not a persuasive study in character. It is stamped with the same brand that defaces all the books discussed in this chapter. It is not sufficiently authoritative to be psychologically interesting; nor does it pose any standard of criticism, moral or social.

All six of the novelists grouped together here as décadents are young. All six juggle words with more than average skill. There are numerous others with equal qualifications for inclusion in their company, but whom I see no point in mentioning. Six are enough!

But what are we to conclude about these writers and their books? The worst error, I think, would be to exaggerate their importance. They do represent a school of literary decadence and it is depressing to see it manifest itself among our youngest literary generation. But I see no reason to believe that these writers speak for anyone save themselves. If they outgrow their present obsession with the aberrations of sex they may conceivably write better, healthier, more significant books. But if they are to do so, they will have to reverse the course on which they have set their steps and for which they have been extravagantly praised in some quarters. They are already so committed to their special variety of hothouse orchids that it is unlikely that they will ever wish to cultivate less exotic flowers.

Probably it would be reasonable to say that such novels as theirs belong to the tradition of Oscar Wilde's *Dorian Gray*. The difference is that today modern freedom of speech and subject matter permits our decadent writers to be far more explicit than their predecessors of the 1890s. And Wilde felt it necessary to give his famous book a conventional moral lesson, a compulsion which his successors do not share. The decadent aesthetes of the 1890s, conspicuous as they were, did not write the enduring fiction of that decade. We should not forget that during the nineties such immortals as Hardy, Meredith, Stevenson, Kipling and Conrad were all at work.

Remembering their achievements should aid us to look on the Capotes and Bowleses with some detachment and perspective; to realize that the books which endure always reflect the vigorous personality of their authors, always concern characters who are interesting and believable, always tell a story capable of holding attention. Verbal necromancy and sexual shocks can never substitute for these qualities, which are basic to good fiction.

VIII

Sensational or Inspirational

"Popularity is a crime from the moment it is sought;
it is only a virtue where men have it whether they
will or no."—*Sir George Savile, Marquis of Halifax*

The sweeping and exaggerated generalization quoted above
represents the opinion of a seventeenth-century statesman who
was thinking in terms of royal courts and national politics. But
it applies with considerable truth to the writing of fiction.
Good, bad and indifferent books can be popular. But the novelist whose deliberate design is to write a popular book rarely
writes a fine one. What kind of novels have been consistently
popular during the last decade?

All kinds, of course. The best-seller lists from 1941 through
1950 include novels by such distinguished writers as Ernest
Hemingway, John P. Marquand and John Hersey. And they
also include in greater numbers sentimental romances by Elizabeth Goudge and Frances Parkinson Keyes and mediocre melo-
dramas by Taylor Caldwell. And the two largest classifications
are, as we should expect, historical novels and religious novels.
Of the one hundred titles listed for that period by the *Publishers' Weekly* eighteen were religious and twenty-nine historical.

There can be little doubt that ever since the publication of *Anthony Adverse* in 1933 historical novels have been the most popular brand of literary merchandise in this country.

Not so long ago a poor but honest youth who was well aware of these facts decided to become a writer. He was ambitious and industrious. And he was not seriously concerned about art or literature. He used to lie awake nights and dream of fame and riches, of the days when his novels would be distributed by book clubs, of their winning enormous cash prizes and leading best-selling lists from coast to coast, of sales to the movies and of being the guest of honor at publicity functions, of addressing women's clubs (for five hundred dollars) and of pretty girls asking for his autograph.

Now this young man was nobody's fool. He prepared a chart and wrote down on it the fruits of some research he had made among best-seller lists. On his chart he plotted out specifications for a supercolossal best seller that would outsell *Gone with the Wind* and make his dreams come true. Among the points he listed were:

1. Great length, so that readers would feel they were getting their money's worth.
2. A simple, dramatic narrative with lots of plot and lots of violent action and a Civil War background.
3. A strong emphasis on spiritual and religious values, so that troubled people could find comfort and solace.
4. A heroine of great strength of character, but one so ruthless, arrogant and sexually abandoned that readers could both admire her and feel morally superior to her at once.

Mixing these ingredients together (without bothering to reconcile points three and four), the young man wrote a book

[123]

which was accepted with alacrity by the first canny publisher to whom it was submitted. But when it was finally published it proved a bust. No one was interested, and the first huge printing had to be remaindered in drugstores at thirty-nine cents a copy. He had left out of his foolproof formula the most essential element of all: an honest belief in the value of what he was doing and in the ideals he preached. Naturally, then, his magnum opus was as synthetic as Spanish architecture on a gasoline station in Maine.

Most unusually popular novelists achieve their popularity because they possess the two basic requirements for it: sincere belief in the traditional moral and social standards of their society and genuine narrative skill. Their style may be crude and their construction clumsy; but they know how to keep their story moving and their readers interested in what will happen next.

This was true of nearly all the most popular novelists of the past. But today a new kind of fictional popularity has been won by novelists specializing in sexual sensationalism. If the young man whose sad story we have just told had put enough episodes based on rape, adultery and promiscuity into his novel he might have achieved the success he longed for. This kind of thing seems to be entirely independent of artistic sincerity. Sexually sensational novels can be manufactured in literary sweatshops by authors who pirate their patterns from other books just as fashion designers pirate models of popular Parisian *coutouriers*. A new and large reading public now exists which makes best sellers of such fare. Surely readers who revel in the works of Kathleen Winsor are not the same as those who are so devoted to Elizabeth Goudge.

Although most novels which achieve great popularity do not

represent the more thoughtful and influential subdivisions of the modern mind, they are an important part of the modern literary scene and consequently are worth at least cursory consideration. They reflect public taste. In fiction the two most popular themes for more than one hundred years have been romantic adventure (today more often than not historical) and religion. The adventure may have a familiar domestic background, in which case it is often a variation on the story of Cinderella; or it may tell of heroic conquests against odds, in which case its resemblance to Jack the Giant Killer is obvious.

Let us consider a typical modern historical novel:

"Tell me a story, Daddy," begged the importunate child. "It must have knights in it and a beautiful princess and lots of fighting and some magic and pirates and harems and torture and white men making savages think they are gods by tricks and cannibalism and treachery and everything else that I like."

The already exasperated father flung the 640-page book he was reading into the fire and began:

"Once upon a time there was a Spanish knight called Alonzo Manrique. He was very brave and very pure. He was shipwrecked on a desolate coast inhabited by cannibal Indians, who put him in a cage to fatten him up. But Alonzo learned two or three Indian languages in a jiffy, escaped and made some other Indians think he was a god by building a wheelbarrow. Finally he joined a Spanish army under Cortez and by his invaluable aid helped it to conquer Mexico."

"But where is the princess and the magic?" demanded the child, who was a stickler for art in its purest form.

"The princess was an Indian princess named Xuchitl, whose father was King Nezahualpilli of Tetzcuco. He had two thousand concubines (never mind, they're what King Solomon had only three hundred of) and a magic heart carved out of jade which made any woman he wanted love him just terribly. Now the princess 'dreamed true' and saw Alonzo in her dreams and loved him and he met her in his dreams and loved her. When she was about to be killed and eaten, who do you think arrived just in time to save her? Why, the young knight, of course! And they recognized each other at once because of their true dreams (no, I don't know how they could do that; they just did). After that they had some terrible adventures. A wicked emperor named Montezuma——"

"You mean the man whose halls the Marines are from?"

"Yes, that's the fellow. Well, he tried to take the princess away from Alonzo but got murdered shortly afterward. So Cortez and his little army and the knight took all his empire for themselves. But Alonzo's poor old mother back in Spain had been thrown into jail by the Inquisition, so the knight and the princess sailed back to help her. But on the way they were captured by pirates and taken to Rabat in North Africa, where Uncle Ned was for a while in the war, and the princess was thrown into a Moorish chief's harem. And you'd never guess how she got out! Why, the chief's favorite wife turned out to be Alonzo's old nurse and she fixed everything up in no time. Soon the princess had a lovely baby boy, but she didn't much like living in Spain. So she and the knight went back to Mexico to help keep the Mexicans from ever getting their own country back."

"Daddy," said the child, who had been looking more and more bored for some time, "that's the silliest story I ever heard. How did you ever make it up?"

"I didn't make it up," replied the long-suffering parent. "I just finished reading it in a monstrous long novel by Salvador de Madariaga. It is called *The Heart of Jade* and I have given you a precisely accurate summary of its plot except for a few details which are hardly fit for grownups to read, let alone little boys. Now beat it."

Salvador de Madariaga is a Spanish scholar, diplomat and biographer of Columbus and Cortez. He knows a great deal about sixteenth-century Spain and a fabulous lot about the conquest of Mexico and the Aztecs. But he doesn't know any more about the writing of creative fiction than the most ordinary historical hack. In fact, he seems to have followed the customary formula of such hacks with slavish fidelity. The formula is something like this:

The mass-production author of historical fiction generally submerges himself for six months or so in a library. He emerges with a prison pallor on his face and an armful of notes on costumes, customs, cooking utensils, battles and the sexual practices usual in a Turkish harem or at the court of Charles II. He then doesn't know what to do with his research, so he puts it down on the even pages of his manuscript and devotes the odd pages to a sensational melodrama about a lusty and willing wench and an unscrupulous roving rascal. The result is a preposterous grafting of research (sometimes scrupulously thorough, more often completely superficial) on a clumsy and mechanical plot.

Every year scores of these synthetic fabrications appear. Sometimes it seems like hundreds. Most of them have an American background. One look at the jackets of these is usually enough to identify them. If the jacket picture shows a woman wearing a *décolletage* more extreme than anything worn by women since the peculiar fashions of ancient Crete, the novel inside is a tale of the Colonial period, and if there is a man in the picture wearing a three-cornered hat it is about the Revolution. If the

[127]

man wears a coonskin cap, it is a buckskin epic of the frontier. And if the jacket shows a pillared portico, the novel is a tale of that paradise on earth, the old South before the war.

Appalled by the mediocrity of such fare, too many critics are inclined to lump them all together. But there are important differences which divide historical fiction into five principal classifications. These are: 1) novels of superficial research and cheaply sensational plots (the majority) of which kindness forbids citing particular offenders; 2) novels based on extensive research but with sensational plots, such as Señor de Madariaga's, or *House Divided* by Ben Ames Williams, or *The Egyptian* by Mika Waltari, or *Forever Amber* by Kathleen Winsor (the most famous, or notorious, of the lot); 3) novels based on sound research and with plots only sufficiently improbable and melodramatic for the legitimate purposes of popular entertainment, such as the works of Thomas B. Costain and Kenneth Roberts; 4) novels based on exhaustive research which make no concessions to popular taste, but which, through lack of creative imagination and technical skill, fail to achieve the rank of important and successful fiction, such as Alice Harwood's *The Lily and the Leopards* or Mary Louise Mabie's *Prepare Them for Caesar;* 5) and the truly fine historical fiction which we will take up in another chapter. Many readers who would appreciate the best historical novels don't read them, confusing the good with the rubbish. And those who delight in the rubbish are incapable of appreciating the best historical novels.

The other outstanding variety of popular fiction, religious novels, has been enjoying a sensational comeback in recent years. As everyone who remembers *Ben-Hur* and *In His Steps* knows, religious novels have always been literary staples. They appeal to millions of persons who are not regular readers of fiction. During the more or less frivolous 1920s and the socially conscious 1930s, however, they were not quite so conspicuously prevalent as they became in the 1940s. Present disasters and fear of things to come undoubtedly stimulated in many readers the desire for a reaffirmation in fiction of deeply cherished beliefs. While the earth shook people found comfort in Franz Werfel's *Song of Bernadette* and food for religious thought in the satirical fantasies and allegories in which C. S. Lewis preached the orthodox doctrines of the Church of England.

Other factors contributed to the fabulous sales of Lloyd Douglas' *The Robe* and *The Big Fisherman*. These pedestrian and clumsy novels may be superficial and inadequate in their picture of the ancient world and inept in characterization; but they possess an authentic narrative drive and a simple and unquestioning Christian faith that make their astounding sales thoroughly understandable. Less amazingly popular, but still spectacularly successful, were Sholem Asch's *The Nazarene, The Apostle* and *Mary*. Written in Yiddish by a Polish-born Jew whose reverence for the Christian story offended many of his orthodox co-religionists, those massive works of profound religious scholarship do not, at first glance, seem to own the stuff of popularity.

They are unrelieved by humor. They have no narrative suspense. They are stuffed with a dense mass of prolix theological disquisition, with the raptures of religious mystics and the hairsplittings of religious dogmatists. In the face of such obstacles why are they popular, and deservedly so?

I think it is because the reverent spirit which infuses them seems truly noble and Mr. Asch himself seems that rare phenomenon, a spiritually minded writer. His books may not fascinate or provide easily swallowed capsules of religious inspiration. But they do inspire respect and admiration. And the thesis of both *The Nazarene* and *The Apostle* is developed with impressive cogency: that Christianity is part of the main stream of Jewish religious thought, its final and culminating development. Everyone does not approve of this idea. But it seems obvious that in these days of hatred and persecution it is welcomed by many.

In the autumn of 1951 a new religious novel by Mr. Asch appeared which was not connected with his Christian trilogy. This was *Moses,* a long, pedestrian and rather unimaginative elaboration of the story of the great lawgiver as it is found in the Bible. With slavish fidelity to the original story, with unquestioning acceptance of every miracle at its face value and with considerable ingenuity in imagining additional details with which to clothe the bare bones of the ancient story, Mr. Asch built up his ponderous novel about Moses himself and about the origin of Jewish ideas of God and righteousness. *Moses* is reverent and scholarly, but prolix and tedious. Nevertheless, at the time of this writing it seems destined to share the vast popularity of its predecessors.

There is another variety of religious fiction currently being written which is only a ripple in the sea of books compared to the tidal wave represented by Lloyd Douglas and Sholem Asch. Since only one example of it, Somerset Maugham's *The Razor's Edge,* was commercially successful, I do not propose to discuss it here. But just for the record we should note that a trend toward mysticism has appeared in the novels of several writers who, like Mr. Maugham, were previously best known for their worldly outlook. The most important and representative of these converts to the mystic way is Aldous Huxley, who tried with small success to express his mystic philosophy in *Time Must Have a Stop*.

The popularity of fiction with a conventional religious theme in the 1940s and the appearance of the less popular religious novels with an unconventionally mystic theme were paralleled by a flood of general books of inspiration and self-help. These offered to make their readers happy and successful by providing simplified short cuts to the wisdom of Freud, the practical success of the sales manager of General Foods and the divine teachings of Christ and the apostles. If most of these nostrums were literary gold bricks for the gullible, superficial and vulgar in the truest sense of the word, they at least appealed to a widespread craving for authoritative help in time of need.

It seems safe to predict that as long as our modern world remains in turmoil, as long as fear and doubt are the constant companions of us all, just so long will the present popularity of religious and inspirational books continue. And it is more than likely that devout religious faith will find expression in a great novel before too many years have passed. The subject is ready and waiting. A vast host of readers can be counted on. All that is required is a novelist of sufficient integrity and skill. Up to the time of this writing religious novelists of sincere faith have not been lacking. What has been missing is a religious writer of major talent in creative fiction.

Although the popular historical novelists and the popular religious novelists have made a profound impression on the bestseller lists of the last decade, we should not overestimate their hold on the reading public. After all, not one of them can even compete with the most popular novelist in American history, a woman whose name is completely forgotten today. But Mrs. Emma Dorothy Eliza Nevitte Southworth, whose life spanned most of the nineteenth century, is still the undisputed champion in point of sales. She wrote more than fifty novels, of which two sold more than two million copies each, and nearly all sold more than a hundred thousand each.

IX

THE ART OF HISTORICAL FICTION:

Richter, Guthrie

"In books lies the soul of the whole Past Time: the articulate audible voice of the Past, when the body and substance of it has altogether vanished like a dream."
—*Thomas Carlyle*

One of the enduring joys of reading is the sense of the past which can be acquired in no other way. Family stories, ancestor worship and sacred heirlooms can inspire only a superficial and often crudely distorted vista backward through the generations. Wider vision and more understanding perception depend on two varieties of books. Histories and biographies provide essential information; fiction provides feeling, the illusion of sharing the experience, the thought and emotion, of the past in spite of barriers of time and death.

Those who live in the present only and are ignorant of, or indifferent to, the past suffer from a variety of intellectual undernourishment. They deprive themselves of much of the meaning of life and of many of its pleasures. One of the most obvious examples of the blight caused by ignorance of the past may be found among travelers. Concord is only another New England village without some knowledge of the great men who lived and

[133]

wrote there. With such knowledge it is a place of pilgrimage. Mount Vernon and Monticello are only old-fashioned country houses to those who have no more than a nodding acquaintance with their distinguished masters.

The apathy and temporal isolation which cut off so many Americans from a knowledge of the past would not exist if enthusiasm for the study of history were general, or if the average popular historical romance were a reliable picture of the period of which it treats. Since neither of these desirable situations exists, the remaining avenue leading to the past, the good historical fiction, deserves more serious attention than it generally receives.

An historical novel, according to my personal definition, is any novel in which the action takes place before the author's birth so that he must inform himself about its period by study. Whether actual historical personages are the protagonists or whether the entire cast is imaginary is irrelevant. What matters is the all-important fact that the author is not writing from personal experience; he is trying to write creative fiction about men and women who lived and loved and died in a world completely different from his own.

It is one of the most difficult of literary tasks. The characters in historical fiction must seem human and interesting; but they must be creatures of their own time, believing many things we no longer believe, feeling emotions we no longer share. One of the many shortcomings of poor historical fiction is the implausibility of the characters. They are either vulgar citizens of the twentieth century masquerading uncomfortably in costume; or they are stiff automatons striking attitudes supposed to be appropriate to their time and place.

The very fact that historical fiction must lean heavily on

research presents serious difficulties to the novelist. He must assume that his readers know little or nothing about the War of the Spanish Succession or the first settlement of North Dakota. But if he tells them all about it in detail he runs the risk of swamping his story with educational exposition. That's what the great inventor of historical fiction did and it's the reason why Walter Scott has few readers today. There is a better, a more subtle and effective way.

It is to plunge the reader into the past without explanations, to let him look at the world of Rameses or Napoleon through the eyes of characters who take that world for granted, to whom everything which seems strange to us is natural and familiar. And then by showing casually what his characters do, what they believe, what customs and conventions they follow, the truly artful historical novelist can lead his readers into the past without interrupting his story to deliver little lectures.

And, as should be obvious, success or failure in historical fiction depends on the same indispensable virtues as are found in all good fiction. A good novel, whatever its time and place, is a story about interesting human beings involved in some kind of conflict or central situation which reveals their characters. Whether the hero wears a rapier and a plumed hat or a sport jacket and no hat is an important detail; but it is not nearly so important as whether he is an interesting individual in whose affairs we can feel lively concern. And always there remains that other all-important individual, who must also be interesting in his personality and his outlook on life, the author.

Those readers and critics who sniff disdainfully at all historical fiction forget, temporarily at least, what a large proportion of the world's acknowledged masterpieces they are scorning. The list includes Tolstoy's *War and Peace,* Hugo's *The Hunch-*

back of Notre Dame, Reade's *The Cloister and the Hearth,*
Thackeray's *Henry Esmond,* Hawthorne's *The Scarlet Letter,*
Melville's *Billy Budd,* Willa Cather's *Death Comes for the
Archbishop,* Elizabeth Madox Roberts' *The Great Meadow,*
Helen Waddell's *Peter Abelard* and many, many others. These
are immortal books. Whether many, or any, of our best contemporary historical novels will achieve similar longevity only
our posterity will know. But that superior work is still being
done in historical fiction I am convinced.

There are two principal ways, it seems to me, in which our
best historical novels reflect the modern mind. The desire to
create a work of art in fiction is, of course, timeless. The desire
to set it against an historical background is personal, springing
both from the emotional lure of the past and the stimulating
artistic challenge presented by it. But the modern serious historical novelist often has two special, topical motives driving
him to his task.

The first of these is the search for historical parallels in the
past which may shed some enlightenment on our perilous present. That's what Arthur Koestler obviously had in mind when
he wrote in *The Gladiators* about the revolt of Spartacus and
interpreted that revolt according to orthodox Marxist teachings
—Mr. Koestler at that early stage in his career had not yet re-
nounced communism. In the same way Herman Kesten would
never have written his *Ferdinand and Isabella* with its terrible
account of anti-Semitic horrors in fifteenth-century Spain if he
himself had not been a refugee from the atrocities of Hitler's
Germany. Other historical novelists have looked at the anguished world about them and written of earlier efforts to
conquer much of mankind, earlier experiments in totalitarianism and earlier struggles for freedom.

The other chief topical motive, I believe, is similar, but less closely linked to current problems. It seems to spring from a natural distaste for the modern world, patriotic pride in the past achievements of our nation, and a sad longing for the simpler world of our ancestors and for the courage, faith and self-reliance of the founding fathers or the pioneers. Some may call this attitude sentimental. But there is much justice in it. Folly, selfishness, weakness and expediency abounded in the past. But, as is always true, there were heroism and nobility, too, and these can be discerned more easily when they are silhouetted against the background of a less complicated and less amorphous age. This kind of feeling is notable in the works of Conrad Richter.

To avoid cluttering this chapter with too many titles, authors and descriptions of books I have relegated a list of notable historical novels to an appendix. Anyone interested in reading further in this neglected field may find a number of my personal favorites listed there. The novels of Conrad Richter and A. B. Guthrie, Jr., are not included, because they are considered here; and neither is Hope Muntz's *The Golden Warrior,* which is discussed in Chapter XV.

Although the American frontier has been one of the dominant forces which shaped our society and although it has been written about in books past all counting, there have been surprisingly few genuinely distinguished novels about it. Among those few I would include Legrand Cannon's *Look to the Mountain,* Elizabeth Madox Roberts' *The Great Meadow,* Willa Cather's *My Antonia,* Conrad Richter's Ohio trilogy and the novels of A. B. Guthrie, Jr.

During the eleven years 1940 through 1950 Conrad Richter wrote six novels. Of these three were slight and disappointing. The other three comprise Mr. Richter's trilogy about the pioneer settlement of Ohio from the first penetration of the forests by seminomadic hunters in the 1780s until the Civil War. *The Trees, The Fields* and *The Town* are certain to rank among the fine novels of our time. Taken together as a vast epic of the American frontier seen in terms of one family they are a majestic achievement. *The Town* won the Pulitzer Prize for fiction in 1950. Few books which have won that award have deserved it half so much.

Conrad Richter's novels all seem to be efforts to convey in words vivid, accurate, emotionally suggestive impressions of important and typical phases in the development of American society. Mr. Richter is a thorough scholar steeped in the lore of the American past. With consummate artistry he writes as if he and his readers both were part of the vanished life of his stories, using the colloquial idioms and special turns of speech of his characters and never departing from their frame of reference.

In the Ohio trilogy Conrad Richter has told the story of Sayward Luckett from childhood to extreme old age. In *The Trees* he described the adventures of the whole Luckett family, "woodsies," of whom Sayward, though only a child, was the bravest, the most responsible and the wisest. *The Fields* continued Sayward's story, telling of her marriage, her many children and the changes in her life which came with the increase of population and the shift from a hunting society to a farming one. *The Town* concluded the chronicle, dramatizing the continued social shifts which were inevitably producing an urban community destined in the near future to become part of an industrial civilization.

Considering the length of the trilogy as a whole, its division into separate episodes and its loose and sprawling structure, it is amazing how emotionally powerful it is. There are wonderfully dramatic and moving stories scattered throughout all three volumes, and wonderfully perceptive full-length portraits of subtly developed characters. There is a rare quality in these glowing pages—the most finished yet unobtrusive artistry, and a profound understanding of the pioneer character as it was manifested in and affected by a way of life now vanished from the earth. These three novels are rich with the special atmosphere of the constantly changing past; and also with a special, intangible atmosphere appropriate to the characters' emotions in various circumstances. Without affectations or stylistic flourishes, Conrad Richter charged his trilogy with intense emotion, an austere but pure and genuinely poetic feeling.

As the climax of *The Town* approaches it becomes apparent that this is not just a superb chronicle of a forest hamlet from the first tree cut down by Sayward's father to the bustling energy of a Civil War city, nor just Sayward's story and that of her husband and children, although it is both of these things. It is also a carefully worked-out and dramatically developed contrast between the diametrically opposed characters of Sayward and her youngest son, Chancey.

Sayward, who had hated the dark and bloody forests of her childhood, who had been taught to read by her own children, was a worker and a fighter, a patient, forgiving, loyal woman. She could forgive the infidelity of her brilliant lawyer husband and some of his deceitful Yankee tricks because she recognized his fine points and because she loved him. She could forgive the weaknesses of her children for the same reasons. Sayward is a persuasively real and extremely sympathetic character— and an heroic one worthy to stand as a symbol of all that was best in the legend of the pioneer woman.

In My Opinion

Chancey was a puny, ailing, timid and imaginative child who could not distinguish between the reality of the world around him and the reality of the daydreams in which he lived much of the time. As a man he was still a dreamer, but an idealist and reformer, tactless, impractical, foolish and contemptuous of the values his mother and other old-timers cherished. His rebellion was a triple one: that of a younger against an elder generation, that of a settled society against the harsh code of the frontier, and that of a visionary idealist against the practical realist. Mr. Richter understands Chancey and even sympathizes with him; but his heart goes out to Sayward.

Like Sayward in her old age, and like Sayward's feckless, forest-vagrant father, Conrad Richter seems to yearn nostalgically for the life of the wilderness, when the world was still as God made it, unspoiled by towns and factories and railroad tracks; and for the simple virtues of the pioneers—courage, loyalty, friendliness and hardihood. This rosy impression of the forest life of the frontier may be one-sided and a little sentimental; but it is an integral part of Mr. Richter's work. He has not overlooked the suffering and privation, the failures and disasters of the pioneers. But the inner core of his trilogy had to be admiring if it was to express, as I believe it does, Mr. Richter's nostalgia for the lost world of the Ohio pioneers.

So the Ohio trilogy is, in its spiritual essence, a muted and mournful lament over time and change, realistic in detail but lyrical in mood. Sayward and Mr. Richter neither deny nor defy the never-ending tide of change; but they don't like it and they are firmly convinced that it would be a good thing for the world if more people met the depressing changes of modern life with the self-reliant grit of the pioneers.

This same feeling, although in less poignant force, is present in the novels of A. B. Guthrie, Jr., *The Big Sky* and *The Way West*. These two magnificent novels, the first about the Mountain Men and the second about the Oregon Trail, comprise the first half of a tetralogy about the Far West on which Mr. Guthrie is now at work. Whatever the merits of the volumes yet to come, those already published qualify their author for a high rank among American writers. Until their publication Western fiction was ninety per cent juvenile melodrama, only ten per cent serious work. And of the ten per cent only the best books of Willa Cather rank with Mr. Guthrie's. Like Conrad Richter, Mr. Guthrie is a profound student of the past about which he writes. And, also like Mr. Richter, he writes in the idiomatic language used by his characters and entirely from their point of view. But, in contrast to Mr. Richter who comes close to poetry in his use of archaic speech, Mr. Guthrie is harsh and gritty and violent. He knows that the early days in the Far West contained much brutality and violence, much living at a primitive level. But he knows with equal conviction that there was inspiring grandeur in the struggle of a few men to conquer a continent. And so Mr. Guthrie's books are romantic in an almost philosophical sense of the word.

The Big Sky is a long, easy-gaited, smooth-running novel which seems unimpressive enough at first, which builds its effects slowly, fitting its separate ideas and episodes together as snugly as the porcupine quills on a buckskin shirt. As one follows Mr. Guthrie's stirring story deeper and deeper into the wilderness, one realizes with increasing certainty that this is not just another combination of research and adventure, that here is a magical re-creation of a lost world and a rare capacity to convey its essential quality. If that sadly overworked word, epic, had not been so debased by indiscriminate misuse, *The Big*

Sky could be called an epic of the Mountain Men. Tarnation! Let's just call it an epic, anyway. How is a word going to get back its proper dignity if we are afraid to use it at all?

This is the story of Boone Caudil, who fetched his pap a lick with a piece of stovewood and so had to light out from the backwoods of Kentucky for the real West. He never stopped until he got to the shining mountains, 'way up past the headwaters of the wide Missouri, where the Crow and the Blackfeet pitched their lodges and the beaver were so thick a trapper never had to bother with coarse fur. Reading *The Big Sky* you can almost smell wet leather and bear grease and buffalo steaks and pine trees and hear the song of the coyotes and feel the cold of the high passes and the heat of the Montana plains in August. Nearly all these things are described as they seemed to Boone, who, in spite of his inarticulate nature, was capable of an abiding passion for the mountain country.

Boone wasn't smart, but he was a wonderful hunter and a crafty Indian fighter. He "thought simple and acted straight and quick." As a free trapper he encountered nearly everything a man could and still keep his scalp. He learned to live on meat and branch water and never even to have any craving for salt or bread or coffee. Boone was a mean man in a fight and he cared more about revenge than most men would think right. But he learned that shooting a man quick doesn't always settle everything; not in the mind it doesn't.

More than his few friends, more than his Indian wife, it was the life of the mountains that Boone loved, "loose and free's ary animal." He loved "the rendezvous and hunting and set-tos with Indians and lonesome streams and high mountains and the great empty places that made a man feel like he was alone and cozy in the unspoiled beginning of things." "This was the way to live, free and easy, with time all a man's own and none to say no to him. A body got so's he felt everything was kin to him, the earth and sky and buffalo and beaver and the yellow moon at night. It was better than being walled in by a house, better than breathing in spoiled air and feeling caged like a varmint, better than running after the law or having the law running after you and looking to rules all the time."

The Big Sky is enough to make the most citified apartment dweller feel the same way, to make him almost wish that the taxi horn in the street was a war whoop and that the towers of Manhattan were the snowy peaks of the Grand Tetons.

In *The Way West* A. B. Guthrie wrote as impressive and final a book about the Oregon Trail as he had about the Mountain Men in *The Big Sky*. Once again he chose an epic theme; for the Oregon Trail from Independence in Missouri to the Cascade Mountains is the great road of the American past. More than the first sites of English settlements in Virginia and New England, more than the memories of the pathfinders who braved the forests of Ohio and Kentucky, it appeals to the national imagination.

The covered wagons rolling across the bare, high plains and through the mountain passes toward a new land and a new life in the immeasurable distance have become symbols of the courage and the hope and the quest for something better, always farther west, which, for lack of a better word, are often called the American dream. The ruts which the iron-rimmed wheels of the prairie schooners cut in the wilderness can still be seen in some places; and they are deep in American literature. But, by some mischance, until *The Way West* there was no notable novel about the Oregon Trail.

The Way West is more restrained and less melodramatic

than *The Big Sky,* more unified in theme and structure, more subtle in its deep understanding of human character. But its material is much more familiar. It lacks the refreshing novelty, the joyful wonder and the exhilarating youthfulness of *The Big Sky.*

This is the story of a band of emigrants, "farmers and town-livers and women and their young, . . . some wantin' to hurry and some to hold back and some scared of Indians and some sorry they set out and some just naturally ornery." They left Independence in the spring of 1845, having elected a captain and a council and having hired an experienced Mountain Man to be their guide. They made it through better than most, with only a minimum of wrangling, sickness and the unavoidable disasters of the road. By the Platte and the Nebraska Coast to Fort Laramie, across the Sweetwater and the Snake with always one more river to cross, through deserts and mountains they plodded on.

They met Kaw and Cheyenne and Sioux and Shoshone; but they were not attacked. They saw buffalo in their millions, "a sight of critters," and escaped being trampled down in a stampede. They knew hunger and exhaustion and hope and near despair. But they met each day's problems as they came, including those inherent in the cantankerous, unpredictable, long-enduring and heroic nature of human beings.

To tell the stories of many people by implication Mr. Guthrie concentrated on the stories of a few, less than a dozen principal characters. Men and women, young and old, good and bad, they are a representative lot. But the most interesting is an easygoing Missouri farmer who developed on the trip from a self-doubting, retiring man into a natural leader, tactful, responsible, patient and strong in what he felt to be right. Mr.

[144]

Guthrie's handling of this difficult psychological theme is impressive and adroit.

With sure skill and absolute command of every detail of equipment, custom, speech and thought, with artful simplicity and eloquent feeling, A. B. Guthrie, Jr., wrote his engrossing and tenderly moving book. He did not pad it to fashionable and excessive length. He did not cheapen it with erotic sensationalism. He did not falsely romanticize or prettify his story —but neither did he conceal his personal feeling that there was indeed something genuinely romantic and inspiring about the great adventure of the Oregon Trail.

Conrad Richter and A. B. Guthrie, Jr., have sought long and diligently for the truth about America's frontier past. And they have put that truth, both to fact and to spirit, into their work with loving care and fine technical skill. Theirs are historical novels which, I believe, will one day be recognized as enduring contributions to American literature. Readers who remain ignorant of their achievement because it is historical deny themselves the rewarding pleasure of acquaintance with two of the finest of contemporary writers.

X

NOVELISTS AND WAR:

Hersey, Michener, Mailer, Jones, Baron, Wouk

"I am tired and sick of war. Its glory is all moonshine.
It is only those who have never fired a shot nor heard
the shrieks and groans of the wounded who cry aloud
for blood, more vengeance, more desolation."
—*William Tecumseh Sherman*

Nearly seven years ago when peace broke out and the first
scattered bits of paper began to flutter lazily in the air over Wall
Street I was standing in Trinity Churchyard looking at the
gravestone of a captain who had fought in the Revolutionary
War. Like the soldiers in Europe, whose victory was at last
won, he too had fought for liberty and honor and what he
believed to be right. A few minutes later when my errand
took me into an office high in the air above the rapidly filling
street, all the stenographers and filing clerks save one were
hanging out the windows emptying wastepaper baskets with
screams and laughter.

An executive of the firm noticed the lone girl sitting at her
typewriter. "You don't have to work any more," he said. "Go
and celebrate with the others."

"Thank you," she said. "I will later, but I'm praying now."

Novelists and War

The guns were being silenced then in Europe and for an interval men dreamed again their ancient dream of peace and good will. But the peace proved to be an impostor and waging it a dismal business. Tyranny and aggression continued to walk the earth and fear of war and enslavement still robbed men of their sleep. A new and more terrible war seemed imminent, today, tomorrow or in ten years. The times were unpleasantly ripe for a harvest of fiction born of the Second World War.

Some of the new crop of war novels appeared before the shooting stopped. Hundreds have appeared since. The young men who wrote them fought in every service and every rank, or reported the war as newspaper or magazine correspondents. Unlike their fathers, who had gone to war with crusading zeal to make the world safe for democracy, they had taken up arms in a spirit of morose stoicism. Their elders had been sure that a better world would emerge from the slaughter and sacrifice of war; and they had been furiously disillusioned when it didn't. The new generation expected nothing and could not be disillusioned in that way. They had read their elders' books. They knew all about the economic consequences of peace and the impotency of the League of Nations.

The older men had expressed their hatred of militarism and their outraged fury inspired by war's horrors, the death and mutilation and agony, which they considered useless. The younger literary generation does not seem to have been so shocked by the grim realities of battle (after all, they had learned about them from able teachers, Hemingway, Remarque, Cobb, Zweig). They are more often stirred to anger by the political ideas about which wars are fought and by the nature of some men as revealed in military organizations and in battle

action. The young war writers do not so much despair because
men slay one another enthusiastically and efficiently; but because so few men understand why they do so, or care; and
because so many worshipers of force and power, so many cruel
and vicious men, were numbered on "our" side as well as on
"theirs."

There are several other differences which seem to divide the
novels of the two World Wars. Those of the First usually concerned one man's experiences. They showed what he endured
and how he reacted emotionally and intellectually. Many of
the new war novels, of course, do the same. But a large proportion are efforts to widen the canvas, to describe the total
experience of war as encountered by a group of representative
characters, or even by a military unit, a squad, a platoon, a whole
regiment. It is all part of the increasingly collective conscious-
ness of the modern mind. Examples of this are Harry Brown's
brilliant novelette, *A Walk in the Sun,* and such less successful
efforts as John Prebble's *The Edge of Night* and Ned Calmer's
The Strange Land.

Other differences are that the young veterans of the Second
World War have taken advantage of the freedom of speech
won by their predecessors and have indulged in an orgy of
soldier obscenity. They have not been content to give a few
examples of the foul speech of barracks and foxholes. They
have, in the name of truth but not of art (which is selective and
suggestive), delighted to rub their readers' noses in verbal filth.
James Jones's *From Here to Eternity* and Norman Mailer's *The
Naked and the Dead* are the two most celebrated examples of
this, both of them major works written in all sincerity.

There are still two other varieties of war fiction currently at
large which were not much in evidence twenty-five years ago.

One of them consists of pretentious and murky dabbling in symbolism, psychology, philosophy and religion with war providing only a dramatic background. Unfortunate examples of this, ambitious efforts which failed as novels, are *An Act of Love* by Ira Wolfert and *The Victory* by Vincent McHugh. The last classification of war fiction seems to be written in flattering imitation of the technique and point of view of Ernest Hemingway. Outstanding examples of this inevitable trend are the well-written and generally superior, but painfully Hemingwayish, novels of Alfred Hayes, *All Thy Conquests* and *The Girl on the Via Flaminia*.

Since most readers of contemporary literature have read widely in the war fiction of both World Wars it seems reasonable to contrast them as a group before taking up a few for closer inspection. The differences we have noted are primarily intellectual and spring from developments which have taken place in the modern mind in one generation. But there is another difference which is caused, I believe, less by conscious convictions than it is by artistic limitations and unconscious predilection. This is the reportorial quality of much modern war fiction.

One feels in reading it that the particular author's real motive is to tell what happened and what it was like, to describe the invasion of a tropical island or the capture of a Norman village. As journalism his book may be quite effective; but it falls short as a work of fiction through failure in the creation of significant characters interesting in themselves, whether in battle action or spending a two-week vacation at Loon Lake. Powers of observation and command of words are sufficient for good journalism, and they are considerable skills which should not be underestimated. But the creation of interesting characters involved in a testing and revealing conflict or situation is another matter, a matter of fictional art.

The reportorial instinct in the writers who emerged from the war is illustrated neatly by John Hersey, who has triumphantly surmounted it, and by James A. Michener, who seems to have succumbed to it completely.

John Hersey was a young reporter on the staff of *Time-Life* when he wrote *Men on Bataan* in 1942. A "quickie" written in the worst excesses of Timese (then more flagrant than it has since become with age and mellowing), this was a hasty account of war in the Philippines and the first of many subsequent efforts to appraise the controversial character of Douglas MacArthur. It revealed nothing of the stature Mr. Hersey was soon to achieve.

A year later Mr. Hersey wrote *Into the Valley,* an account of a Marine patrol in the jungles of Guadalcanal which revealed for the first time how brilliant a reporter he is. His eye for significant detail and his uncanny skill in letting facts speak for themselves without editorial comment gave this little book an authentic impact matched by few other examples of war reporting. He used the same stark simplicity in his celebrated *Hiroshima,* which was published in 1946.

This powerful and terrible little book told of the destruction of the Japanese city by the first atomic bomb used in war as Mr. Hersey reconstructed it from the personal stories of six survivors. Without even raising his voice to scream of horrors, by just setting down what happened to his six characters, Mr. Hersey moved the hearts of many thousands of readers, readers whose mixed emotions included appalled shock at the monstrous new force let loose by their government and an uneasy sense of guilt that the atomic bomb had been used at all when the Japanese war was so nearly won.

But before he wrote *Hiroshima* Mr. Hersey had demonstrated in *A Bell for Adano,* which was published in 1944, how successfully he could dramatize the issues of war in fictional terms. And those issues have been better understood by our contemporary war writers than were the equally real but not quite so portentous issues of the earlier conflict. War writers as gifted as Mr. Hersey have been able to look beyond both horrors and heroics and record a wider, deeper truth of war.

Adano was an obscure village in Sicily, one of the first overrun by invading Americans and put under American Military Government administration. When Major Victor Joppolo took charge in the town hall he inquired what were the town's most immediate needs. A few answered bread, more answered a bell. The ancient, historic and beloved town bell had been shipped away to be melted into cannon for Mussolini. The citizens of Adano wanted it back. It was a symbol of peace, and of old, familiar, decent ways of doing things. They felt lost without it. Major Joppolo was the kind of man who could understand that bread alone is not enough; that bells can have an equal importance.

A Bell for Adano is the story of Major Joppolo's brief career in Adano. But it is far more than that. It is also a parable about war and human nature and democracy and fascism, and the frightful risks and responsibilities of military conquest.

Victor Joppolo was a first-generation Italian-American. He was a modest and unassuming man, tactful and patient, delighted at the chance to put his knowledge of Italian to good use in aiding the democratic cause as he understood it. He is that rare thing, a hero who is a genuinely good man and at the same time a believable and likable one. The major was an idealist, but he was also a practical man with plenty of worldly knowledge. He knew well that all the "bad men" were not on the opposing side, that there were too many unlabeled fascists in American uniforms.

Although Mr. Hersey based his novel on the story of an actual person and an actual incident involving a bell and the brutal arrogance of General George Patton, he transmuted his raw material of facts into an integrated and intensely human novel filled with the warm glow of his respect and affection for human beings. The result is an engrossing, humorous and somber book. The major put his democratic creed as simply as this: "I want you to be happy together. I want all of you to have as much as you can of what you want, without hurting anyone else. That is what I want in Adano." And that is what we all should want for the world. It might help a little to get it if enough millions of people shared Major Joppolo's and Mr. Hersey's simple faith.

A Bell for Adano was one of the first fine war novels. It is still one of the best. But it is slight in comparison to Mr. Hersey's greatest achievement, *The Wall,* a novel of such scope and grandeur that it transcends the limitations of war fiction. It will be considered separately in Chapter XV.

James A. Michener's postwar literary output now includes four books, of which *Tales of the South Pacific,* the first, is immeasurably the best. A former merchant sailor, publishing-house editor and writer of educational books, Mr. Michener enlisted in the Navy as an apprentice seaman and left it as a lieutenant commander. Although he modestly says that he was "only a paper-work" sailor, he learned to know every island from New Guinea to New Zealand where young Americans fought or just waited out the war. In *Tales of the South Pacific* he collected eighteen loosely linked short stories about them.

They were amazingly good, fresh, simple and expert in their presentation, humorous, engrossing and even moving. They all were distinguished by an unusual combination of thoughtful insight appealing to mature minds and old-fashioned storytelling, which made the most of exotic local color. Mr. Michener was adroit in his manipulation of the dramatic possibilities of men at war on tropical islands; but he also dug deeply into the character and behavior of young Americans in fantastic circumstances and made by implication many a pointed comment on courage, boredom, discipline, love and sex.

Tales of the South Pacific contains several excellent narratives of battle action; but it is not primarily about combat. Its fundamental purpose seems to be to fuse the functions of reporting and fiction, to use the methods of fiction to tell American civilians about war in the South Pacific, the way men lived and thought and felt on isolated staging islands, at great Navy shore bases, deep in the jungles of the Solomons.

Comic, satirical, romantic and exciting by turns, Mr. Michener's tales are tough but not hysterically so, realistic about single men in barracks, but not intended to shock. They are too well-balanced for that. And they are illuminated by his profound admiration for courage, generosity, patience, kindliness and humor.

James Michener's second book, a semiautobiographical novel called *The Fires of Spring,* bears all the earmarks of being a first novel which was published second only by accident. Although it is written in immensely readable fashion and contains a gallery of vivid and amusing minor characters, it is overly emotional, confused and confusing. When Mr. Michener describes the swindling tricks of amusement parks or the horrors of life on the Chautauqua circuit, he writes vigorously and well, the instinctive reporter in him doing a good job. But when he describes the ethical equivocations of his sensitive young hero he loses his way in a maze of words, and loses his readers' interest, too. Somehow he has not been able to turn his youthful experience into successful fiction as he has the war experience of his maturity.

In *Return to Paradise* Mr. Michener invented a hybrid literary form, which consists of alternating excellent travel articles with short stories designed to dramatize the conditions described in the articles. As journalism, *Return to Paradise* is outstanding, a fine account of the postwar South Pacific crowded with concrete information and significant anecdotes. But the quality of the stories is much inferior to that of the reporting and much inferior, also, to that of the stories in *Tales of the South Pacific*. The evidence is piling up that as Mr. Michener becomes more expert as a journalist he is becoming less effective as a writer of fiction. There is no harm in that. We need journalists as good as Mr. Michener. But those who were excited by the appearance of the wonderful tales cannot help being disappointed.

And then in the autumn of 1951 came Mr. Michener's fourth book, a volume with no fictional element at all. *The Voice of Asia* is good, popular, topical reporting. But it seems a plain indication of which fork in the road Mr. Michener has chosen.

The two most celebrated American war novels, *The Naked and the Dead* by Norman Mailer and *From Here to Eternity* by James Jones, are both remarkable examples of powerful writing by greatly gifted young men, and of almost adolescent sensationalism, lack of restraint and lack of a sense of artistic proportion.

The Naked and the Dead is almost overwhelming in its ability to convey the terrible urgency of battle, the chilling excitement, the stupefying exhaustion, the tension, fear and despair. The horrors of war have seldom been rendered more brilliantly. But Mr. Mailer lays equal emphasis on the characters of a dozen men, all, save two officers, members of the same squad. With great skill, with revealing dialogue and expert stream-of-consciousness passages, he shows what kind of men they are and how they react to the pressure of battle, to the impact of one another's personalities and to the lure of power and command. All this is extremely well done. *The Naked and the Dead* is a harrowing and psychologically interesting novel, but one with several serious shortcomings.

One of them is some murky and ambiguous symbolism which serves little positive purpose. Another is Mr. Mailer's Marxist picture of American civilizaton. Of his large cast only two are educated men and they are a fascist general and a weakling lieutenant. His GIs, without exception, are victims of society, ignorant, poor, callow, stupid and foul-mouthed. They are adequately brave and Mr. Mailer respects them and even likes them. But he insists that they all come from unhappy families, that none of them knows anything about fidelity in love, that all of them are primitive creatures barren of ideas and ideals.

No one questions that some Americans are like this. But everyone knows that many are not. In any representative group there are decent and reasonably intelligent men. The United States Army did not consist solely of brutes and morons. To make his criticism of American society Mr. Mailer indulges in grotesque exaggeration. The Lord destroyed Sodom because

[155]

there were not so many as ten righteous men in the city. Mr. Mailer with equally sweeping condemnation found no righteous men in the United States Army.

Soon after the publication of *The Naked and the Dead* a great debate arose over its profusion of profanity, obscenity and sexuality. That Mr. Mailer erred artistically in this respect I feel certain. In the middle of this outspoken century no normal adult has any illusions about the nature of soldier talk. But enough is enough. His tireless repetitions were tasteless and tedious. But, I am convinced, they were an honest mistake made in the name of realism. Some months after *The Naked and the Dead* was published I received the following letter and printed it and my reply in the *New York Times*. The points made apply equally well to James Jones's *From Here to Eternity*.

Louisville, Ky.
Dec. 8, 1948.

Dear Mr. Prescott:

I have just observed your name among the list of persons recommending *The Naked and the Dead* by Norman Mailer. I have read most of the book.

My purpose in writing this letter is a latent curiosity to learn, if possible, why a man of your standing and connections would recommend a book containing such filth. Of what earthly benefit could it be to society, or to an individual reading it? How could one read this book without a feeling of revulsion?

For instance, if you had a daughter in her teens, would you like to have her read it? Would you feel proud if she said: "Daddy, did you recommend this book?" Could you defend your actions?

Sincerely,
GRANT MASON

Novelists and War

Dear Mr. Mason:

Your letter seems to me to be based on several misunderstandings of the function of literature. But, since you speak for a point of view still widely held in spite of many victories won against it during the last hundred years, I will try to answer you.

First, then, I recommended *The Naked and the Dead* because I believe it to be a remarkable work, dramatic, powerful, honest and moving; a successful transformation of war experience into creative fiction. I know of no other novel about the recent war of comparable importance.

It is quite true that it would have been much improved by drastic editing, by condensation and greater selectivity. Mr. Mailer lacks taste, judgment and maturity. But he is young and he is greatly gifted. It is true that his characters are not a fair cross section of American life. They are frighteningly primitive and generally deplorable. But it is the artist's privilege to choose his subject matter, the novelist's to write about what he pleases. It is lamentably true that in his effort to report faithfully the obscenity of soldier speech Mr. Mailer did so to unfortunate excess.

But all this cannot change the fact that Mr. Mailer wrote an exceptional book which deserves to be recommended to all readers of serious fiction, to everyone interested in knowing about America's participation in the Pacific war and to all who watch for the emergence of promising literary talent.

You ask how *The Naked and the Dead* could benefit society or the individual? There are two logical answers. The first is that a social or individual benefit is a hard thing to judge and depends on where you are standing in relation to what fence. Many people feel that greater knowledge about the true nature of our less privileged, less cultivated fellow citizens is a step toward substantial benefit.

The second answer is that there can be no such criterion applied to fiction. Did Mr. Pickwick benefit anyone except by

amusing him? Did *The Red Badge of Courage* benefit anyone
except by increasing his vicarious experience and so his knowledge of life? Fiction written to uplift is rarely good fiction.
The primary purpose of fiction is to tell a story, to create people
and to interpret life according to the author's vision of it.

How could one read *The Naked and the Dead* without a
feeling of revulsion? I don't know. I was revolted, too. But
much human behavior, as our tragic century so plainly shows,
is revolting. To be revolted may be a healthy thing.

Your question about a teen-age daughter seems to me to be
based on a particularly erroneous premise. A girl of seventeen
(shall we say?) presumably knows the facts of human biology
and that many men behave badly and use vile speech. I think
that she would react to *The Naked and the Dead* in one of two
ways. Either she would dislike it intensely and read only a little
or she would become absorbed in its terrible picture of war and
read it all. In either case, I don't think that the obscenities, after
their first shock, would matter much. They are not attractive.
They could never make anyone wish to use a similar vocabulary.

Since Flaubert wrote *Madame Bovary,* and probably for long
before that, efforts have been made to suppress books because
they describe behavior which everyone knows to be commonplace. Would-be censors forget that no one can be demoralized
by knowledge or by mere words. You do not have to read any
book. Unless you are tied down while someone reads out loud,
you read from choice.

Our daughters have to live in this world. As much as their
share of free will allows they have to decide what kind of
women they are going to be. They might well begin by decid-
ing not to be the kind of women Mr. Mailer's soldiers talked
about with such enthusiasm.

It would be artistic death to reduce all fiction to the insipid
level of *Little Women* just because there are innocent young
people in the world. There are adults, too. Innocence based on

ignorance is a poor thing compared with decency based on deliberate decisions in favor of honorable behavior.

Let those who are interested, as you yourself were, read *The Naked and the Dead*. Those who are not can ignore it, or stop reading it on page two.

Sincerely yours,

ORVILLE PRESCOTT

Three years after the publication of *The Naked and the Dead,* Mr. Mailer's second novel appeared. It was a political parable called *Barbary Shore.*

Although *Barbary Shore* contains flashes of brilliant descriptive writing, it is a miserable disappointment. A tale of six characters in a Brooklyn rooming house, it is a sad mélange of indirection, obscurity, symbolism and dismal boredom. Beneath its cryptic and mannered writing a political message lies and that message seems to be a plea for an anti-Stalin, Trotskyite brand of communism. If it isn't, Mr. Mailer has only himself to blame. Obscurity and politics make a poor mixture, especially when the politics are so lamentable. Norman Mailer is richly talented. If, with greater maturity, he acquires artistic self-discipline and political maturity he may yet go far.

There are 858 pages and 430,000 words in *From Here to Eternity.* That's nearly five times as long as the average novel. But this block-buster of a book is several times as interesting as the average novel. This powerful and brutally shocking novel packs a dynamic punch. Its narrative drive is tremendous, its intensity of emotion contagious, its soldier characters are solidly real and interesting. But it, too, is marred by grievous faults. Its only two women characters are preposterous. Its concentration on the worst conceivable aspects of peacetime army life just before Pearl Harbor is so exclusive that it seems both hysterical and sentimentally exaggerated. It is too long, too repetitious and too drenched in obscenity and eroticism.

The United States Army is no country club. Military discipline can be stupid and wretchedly abused. But still, the best-fed, best-paid soldiers in the world, living in Hawaii before the bombs fell, with frequent access to the bars and brothels of Honolulu, were not in the worst circumstances imaginable. There is a strain of neurotic self-pity in Mr. Jones's writing which contributes to the emotional tension of his book, but which does seem definitely immature. And this, too, may be one of the elements of the modern mind which crop out in our war fiction.

From Here to Eternity is the story of the decline and fall of a soldier, broken and destroyed by army life, which he loved, and by the army system, which he hated. Robert E. Lee Prewitt, a miner's son from Harlan County, Kentucky, was the best bugler in the regiment, an expert boxer and a fine soldier. He was fiercely proud, stubbornly independent and incorruptibly honorable according to his own instinctive, confused notions. He was also young, foolish, ignorant and violently emotional. How the army drove Prewitt into desperate and futile rebellion, and then into becoming an alcoholic, a deserter and a murderer, is James Jones's story.

The really shocking thing in *From Here to Eternity* is not its language and its explicit sexuality. It is its account of Prewitt's persecution. Prewitt had blinded a man in boxing and refused to box any more. But regimental glory required that so able a boxer fight for the outfit.

Personal meanness, intrigue and favoritism can be expected everywhere in life. But that the gigantic power of a military

[160]

organization should be used in contradiction of its own laws to break one individual standing up for his rights is a travesty of decency. Mr. Jones leaves few doubts that such a thing could happen. And when he describes the sadistic tortures inflicted in the punishment "stockade" he leaves his sickened and enraged readers wondering how much American army practices duplicate those of the totalitarian nations.

From Here to Eternity is raw and brutal and angry, too violent a book for literary finesse and subtlety. But it is not just an explosion of talent. In spite of its faults and excesses it is a considerable achievement. James Jones, like Norman Mailer, needs only to mature in objective judgment and artistic restraint to become a first-rate novelist.

In refreshing contrast to the emotional bitterness and verbal violence of Mr. Mailer and Mr. Jones are the superb (and in this country little appreciated) novels of Alexander Baron, a young Englishman who served for six years in the infantry, seeing action in Sicily, Italy and France. Far more temperate and mature in outlook, far more tightly constructed, they bear eloquent testimony to the fact that Mr. Baron possesses the two basic literary virtues: affectionate understanding of human beings and technical mastery of the art of fiction.

In *From the City, from the Plough* Mr. Baron wrote the story of the six hundred men who comprised the Fifth Battalion of the Wessex Brigade. Its first half describes training in England in the spring of 1944, its second the invasion of Normandy.

There are no heroes in these tough and stirring pages, only men: cockneys from the London slums, outcasts from the docks of Liverpool, farmers from the west counties, beribboned veterans from the desert war. Their language is foul, but Mr. Baron spares his readers the worst of it. They are enormously interested in drink and women; but Mr. Baron has the wisdom to recognize that they are interested in other things, too: in families, jobs, friendships and even in ideas. Ordinarily fallible, ignorant, frightened, they are intensely human, sometimes heroic. Caught in a disaster beyond their understanding, they intone their incantation, "Roll on, the peace!" and fight and die until there are only a few score left.

It is remarkable in *From the City, from the Plough* how Mr. Baron crams so much into so little space. There isn't much about army life or about battle which he doesn't take care of. He writes of war and of his fellow soldiers with the intimate knowledge of long acquaintance. He knows that some men are cruel and that many are stupid and lazy and self-centered. But he is not bitter or surprised. Many other men are brave and kindly and loyal.

That war is abominable Mr. Baron makes clear. But sometimes it is a necessary abomination, a lesser evil, and so he does not scream about it in childish temper tantrums. He writes quietly, gently about the noisiest, least gentle thing in the world. And by his very restraint he adds to the sorrow and pity which are the dominant impressions of his masterly little book.

One of Mr. Baron's most intelligent soldiers says with melancholy irony, "Such a lot of fuss about such a little river!" His irony lies in the fact that he knows well the fuss isn't just about a little river; it is about the destiny of mankind.

From the City, from the Plough is about the behavior of men at war and the nature of war itself. But a lot of war is waiting, waiting behind the lines for the orders which will mean action again, waiting and drinking and making love in the immemorial way of soldiers. It is about this aspect of war which Mr. Baron writes in his second novel, *Wine of Etna.*

This is a story about battle-worn men relaxing, and of the slum dwellers of the Sicilian town of Catania who help them to do so. Ribald, humorous, compassionate, occasionally grim, *Wine of Etna* is as compactly written and as intimately authentic as it predecessor. Mr. Baron does not overlook any of the misery and corruption of war. But his primary attention is always focused on basically decent and sorely tried human beings seeking a morsel of happiness, a moment of forgetfulness, an illusion of love in a world gone mad. Taken together, these two short books seem to me to offer one of the most complete, most objective and most poignantly true accounts of war in all modern fiction.

It is impossible to mention more than a few of the most representative war novels without expanding this already swollen chapter out of all proportion. But there is one more notable book which it would be a critical sin to omit. This is *The Caine Mutiny* by Herman Wouk, a long novel about the United States Navy and two psychologically fascinating officers, Ensign Willie Keith and Lieutenant Commander Philip F. Queeg.

Although it contains numerous scenes of exciting action in the Pacific, *The Caine Mutiny* is not primarily about battles at sea. It is a novel about the navy itself as an institution with practices and traditions peculiar to itself—about rank and discipline, about human character in an unfamiliar environment and about a dramatic crisis which arises when naval command is entrusted to an officer incapable of exercising it properly.

Willie Keith was a likable, ordinary, decent and intelligent young man whose growth from foolish adolescence to responsible maturity in the pressure of war and of life on the destroyer-minesweeper *Caine* under Queeg is always a convincing and interesting process. But far more dramatic is the case of Queeg.

A giggling martinet, a stupid, inefficient, lazy and cowardly weakling, he was a petty tyrant and general menace. But was he only an oppressive eccentric who should be endured in patience, or was he a psychopath far gone in paranoia? On that question hung the justification of the mutiny which is the crux of *The Caine Mutiny*. Mr. Wouk develops it extremely well, with racy wit and genial humor, with lively pace and much ingenuity of incident, and with unexpected subtlety.

When the chips were down Queeg turned out to be a pathetic as well as a contemptible character. Issues were more complicated on the *Caine* than they at first appeared. Maybe the mutiny wasn't justified after all. Maybe the rigid codes of the navy made more sense than they seemed to. All these matters gave young Willie Keith food for furious thought. Mr. Wouk writes of them objectively as well as dramatically, without moralizing, always keeping his novel an entertaining and expert story—but with the provocative ideas always present, too. *The Caine Mutiny* is unnecessarily long. But, save for that one fault, it is an impressive book, mature, astute and constantly entertaining.

The Caine Mutiny is a war novel without bitterness, disillusion, obscenity, atrocities or corruption. We may be thankful that such cool intelligence, such well-balanced judgment and such diverting humor can be found in one of the best novels yet written out of war experience by an American.

XI

SATIRISTS:

Waugh, Marquand

"Difficile est satiram non scribere."—Juvenal

Although there are no reliable statistics about the prevalence of satire in fiction, it should be plain to even the most casual reader that satire has never been the favorite medium of many distinguished novelists. But of those who have found satire congenial to their temperaments a number have been distinguished indeed. We have only to recall that Cervantes, Rabelais, Swift, Voltaire, Peacock, Meredith and Mark Twain all wrote satirical novels to feel properly respectful about so important a variety of literary expression.

The only definitions of satire I have been able to come by seem to me grossly inadequate insofar as they pertain to fiction. So I have been obliged to define it myself. Satire, then, is the expression of moral or social criticism by means of fantasy, exaggeration or humor. It always implies the existence of superior standards of conduct or higher levels of intelligence than those of the persons satirized. Satire springs from conviction. If it gives vent only to personal pique or private fury through sarcasm, burlesque or abuse it is not true satire.

Today fictional satire is generally directed at social classes or occupational groups, sometimes at particular individuals. Its criticism may be affectionate, gentle and understanding. Often it is vitriolic.

During the last few years a number of satirical novels of a similar nature appeared, and a fictional pattern emerged for what, in want of a better name, might be called the New York novel. The typical New York novel has nothing to say about most of the people who live and work in New York. Its cast is composed of the talented, the famous, the successful and the newly rich. Its scene is midtown Manhattan, Park Avenue and Sutton Place, Greenwich Village and Times Square, Radio City and Madison Avenue, assorted bars and bedrooms. Its world is dedicated to the cult of cold careerism and its point of view is disgusted if not nauseated.

Some New York novels are as honest and able as John Brooks's *The Big Wheel,* which concerned ethical issues among the editors of a famous magazine. Some are as spiteful examples of the keyhole-and-transom school of subliterature as Ralph Ingersoll's *The Great Ones.* Some are as crude and even ludicrous as Frederic Wakeman's *The Hucksters,* which satirized radio advertising, or as savagely witty as Dawn Powell's *The Locusts Have No King,* which lampooned New York's "success clique." Some are as violent as Charles Yale Harrison's *Nobody's Fool,* which tore a public-relations expert limb from limb. And some are as angry and mechanical as Laura Z. Hobson's *The Celebrity,* which mocked the cult of gossip-column fame.

New York novels have paid their discourteous respects to the theater, the movies, the publicity business, all three varieties of publishing (book, magazine and newspaper), and to advertising, especially to advertising. Most of them have been fashionably tough and fashionably "liberal" in their politics, adequately witty and competently readable. But more often than not there has been a hollow ring in their attacks on the streamlined vulgarity and chromium-plated cynicism of their authors' former social and professional associates. Unworthy suspicions raise their ugly heads that perhaps those grapes are sour. The authors' righteous wrath seems adulterated by considerable fascination with the excitement, glitter and tinsel glamour of the life they affect to scorn. And consequently the cutting edge of their satire is blunted.

Although personal pique and exaggerated fury are generally the rule in the New York novels there is at least one delightful exception. This is *Home Town* by Cleveland Amory, who had previously made himself moderately famous as the author of *The Proper Bostonians*. A Proper Bostonian himself, Mr. Amory proved in *Home Town* that he knew New York as well as Boston, and that he could ridicule cynicism, careerism, lion hunting and lust for publicity with wit and cheerful gaiety. *Home Town* is the story of an intelligent but naïve young Westerner lost in the New York jungle of pretense and insincerity. Since Mr. Amory's Westerner was a writer and most of his adventures took place in publishing circles, *Home Town* is particularly amusing as a genial satire of the more outrageous lunacies of the literary life.

Several New York satires ridiculed individuals easily identified by anyone familiar with the particular milieu concerned. And most of them were crude and superficial in characterization. Their casts contained too many straw men erected for the sole purpose of being knocked down. The result of all this is that contemporary satire in fiction has not deserved to be taken very seriously.

But there are two modern satirists who are such accomplished men of letters that their rank among the foremost living novelists seems indisputable. One of them is English and one American. They are Evelyn Waugh and John P. Marquand.

For many years Evelyn Arthur St. John Waugh was regarded as one of the cleverest of the younger English novelists. It wasn't until the publication of his *Brideshead Revisited* in 1945, when Mr. Waugh was not so young any more, that he was generally recognized as being far more than a clever writer of satiric comedy. That brilliant novel demonstrated once and for all that he is an expert craftsman in fiction, a fine stylist and a shrewd manipulator of character. And it showed also how tenaciously he clings to a rigidly fixed set of opinions about life in the modern world.

Before the publication of *Brideshead Revisited* it was difficult to know how seriously to take the impudent novels of this scornful and frighteningly sophisticated aristocrat. His satirical, semifarcical, outrageously amusing charades ridiculed the pretensions, hypocrisies and immoralities of English society with poisonous dexterity. They were wonderfully entertaining, dryly comic in a haughty and malicious fashion.

The ingenuity of comic invention, the irrepressible gaiety and caustic malice of such books as *Decline and Fall, A Handful of Dust* and *Black Mischief* were as exhilarating as a ride on an amusement-park roller coaster, and left one about as breathless. These, and the other books like them, shone with a fine polish as bright as an apple's that has just been wiped on the seat of a peddler's pants; but wasn't there something shrill and effete about them, something which repelled while their wit attracted?

In *A Handful of Dust* Mr. Waugh mocked immorality in privileged circles with caustic cruelty. But he mixed so much

[168]

sheer buffoonery with his bitter sallies from his citadel of traditional values that the result was an incongruous hodgepodge.

Black Mischief, a lunatic farce about an imaginary kingdom much like Ethiopia, was funny, satirical, absurd and erotic. But it was too venomous to be just comic light entertainment, too grotesque and foolish to be really effective in its satire. It was marred by a spiteful sort of snobbery which found people funny just because they were Anglican bishops, Armenian traders or benighted natives.

If Evelyn Waugh had never written anything else than these early satires his reputation would still be substantial. So marvelously deft an entertainer cannot be ignored. The mere fact that his satirical point of view was rarely clear, ranging as it did from righteous condemnation to irresponsible drollery, could not detract from the wit and the glitter of his books. But with *Brideshead Revisited* Mr. Waugh clarified his position, and with his subsequent books he has maintained it with inflexible determination.

As a novelist Mr. Waugh instinctively writes satiric comedy; but as a critic of the modern world he expresses a personal philosophy compounded of his aristocratic, conservative political convictions and of his Roman Catholic religion. Although Mr. Waugh became a Catholic convert sometime in the early 1930s, his new faith was not immediately apparent in all his books. Chiefly present in a biography of Edmund Campion, a Catholic martyr executed for treason in the reign of Queen Elizabeth, it did not noticeably color his fiction until *Brideshead Revisited.*

That brilliant tour de force is still the high point of Mr. Waugh's career, a novel with a clearly stated theme and point of view, in addition to his usual satiric thrusts and outbursts of sophisticated and urbane horseplay. It is also his only novel in which the characters are subtly and elaborately developed. Its prose alone is a pleasure to read, cool and controlled, flexible and graceful, sharp and incisive. But occasionally its impeccable sheen is marred by elaborate similes several sentences too long which stick up like sore thumbs beautifully bandaged in watered silk.

The dialogue of *Brideshead Revisited* is excellent, witty, fluent, natural; and is superbly used to reveal the speakers' characters. The satire is almost feline in its playful savagery; but somehow its cold detachment is so great that the sting doesn't last long. And a year after the conclusion of the Second World War the extravagant follies of English society, the decadence and shallowness of the world of art, fashion, politics, money and vice of the 1920s and 1930s, seemed like a pretty dead dog to be beaten with such elegance.

This is the story of Charles Ryder, of his youth and his intricate relationships with the family of the Marquis of Marchmain. All the members of that futile and fastidious family were rich, clever, frustrated, self-indulgent and unhappy. Remembering them, Charles felt a strange nostalgia for a more distant past, not just for that of his youth, but for a time when aristocracy was more responsible, when order and traditional values had not vanished from the earth. He shrank from the present "where wealth is no longer gorgeous and power has no dignity." This natural yearning of Charles (and of Mr. Waugh) is not just an expression of intellectual and moral snobbery (although it is tinged with that); it is a basic part of their philosophy, their protest against the twentieth century.

If the point of view of *Brideshead Revisited* is fastidious detachment, its theme is religious. The members of the Marchmain family were not only arrogant aristocrats; they were also Roman Catholics. Mr. Waugh writes in the person of Charles Ryder as an agnostic. But the unbelieving Charles was acutely aware of the importance to the Marchmains of their faith, how it arched across the universe of their thought and action. When various Marchmains drifted from the teachings of their Church, or tried to live without them, they invariably came to grief, repented their erring ways and found peace only in the faith of their fathers.

In the Marchmain family Mr. Waugh paints a picture of Catholicism in decay; and by showing the evils of such decay and the need of the Marchmains to revitalize their religion and to abide more closely by its precepts he emphasizes what he believes is a need of all men. *Brideshead Revisited* is a satire of worldly and corrupt behavior written to teach orthodox Catholic doctrines.

But Mr. Waugh's next two books, both of them short satires of deplorable aspects of modern civilization, show no signs of similar concern with a major theme, or even with subtly realized characters. *The Loved One* is a thoroughly gruesome and fiendishly entertaining attack upon the horrors of life in Southern California. *Scott-King's Modern Europe* is a less amusing, but still moderately effective blast at the Communist variety of totalitarianism.

Rarely in fiction have such execrably bad taste and such cruel wit been combined as they are in *The Loved One.* This is not a book which the squeamish or queasy of stomach can face with composure. Its humors are ghoulish; its hyena laughter snarls obscenely. Mr. Waugh was never more brilliant. But somehow he leaves the impression that he has fired a sixteen-inch broadside at a target which could have been disabled as well with a harpoon. The excesses he mocks hardly deserve so obliterating an attack.

Although Mr. Waugh leaves some fairly deep wounds in the much scarred flanks of the movie business and wickedly impales the British celluloid colony (pukka sahibs bravely maintaining imperial prestige among the barbarians), he concentrates his heaviest fire on the outlandish follies of the mortuary business. By the time he has finished with the sanctimonious, sentimental, hypocritical, mercenary and vulgar practices of "Whispering Glades" he has produced a mordant mixture of farce and indignation.

The Loved One derives its title from the only term used to describe the dead at "Whispering Glades." The evasive phrase symbolizes the false view of life which Mr. Waugh finds so utterly repellent. A deliberate effort to smother reality under trappings of irrelevant decoration and to distort values so that comfort, conformity and a perpetual adolescent euphoria pass for the true goals of life arouses his nauseated contempt. This, he seems to say, is true decadence, worse than more conventional corruption.

Satire at its most ferocious, *The Loved One* is a macabre frolic filled with laughter and ingenious devices. Devilishly clever and impishly amusing, it is a fictional exaggeration of an actual institution and state of mind which are fanciful exaggerations to begin with.

In *Scott-King's Modern Europe* Mr. Waugh writes with equal distaste of an infinitely more serious subject. But since Communist tyranny has been analyzed at length in many better books as well as almost daily in the newspapers his results are not so striking.

The last book to come from Evelyn Waugh's fertile and facile pen is a complete departure from his earlier work. *Helena* is a historical novel about the saint who was the mother of the Emperor Constantine and the legendary finder of the True Cross. Slight, exquisitely written, gently humorous, this pale and graceful story is neither a chronicle of a violent epoch nor a serious study in character. Mr. Waugh calls it a legend and that's what it is, a charming one with few of the more substantial merits of superior fiction. Parts of it center about abstruse points of Catholic doctrine which are just suggested, but not explained to the uninitiated.

Whether *Helena* is an indication that Evelyn Waugh is on the point of forsaking the satire which won him international fame for more specifically religious subjects only time will tell. It may be; for in conversation with me shortly after its publication in 1950 he said that he regarded it as his best book; in fact, that he liked it so much he had read it twenty times! In any case, we may feel certain that Mr. Waugh will not compromise with the modern world he despises and that he will continue to express his allegiance to the ordered, older, more gracious codes of the aristocratic past and to the ancient religion he professes. Mr. Waugh's reaction to the modern mind is to refuse to have anything to do with it.

Most of Evelyn Waugh's novels are glossily clever, but without depth. It is one of the measures of John P. Marquand's distinction that he is one of the most brilliantly entertaining novelists of his century and also a profound student of character and society. I believe that no modern American novelist can match Mr. Marquand's achievement. Some have written novels as good as his (notably James Gould Cozzens), but none has written so many fine ones.

In My Opinion

John Phillips Marquand, a "fiction writer since 1921" according to his *Who's Who* biography, is the author of some 125 magazine stories and of nineteen books. Since the publication of *The Late George Apley* in 1937 his place in the front rank of American literature has been secure. Seven more notable books have followed that masterpiece without a single letdown in quality. All of them are about the wellborn or the well-heeled, the economically fortunate—whether withered members of Boston's aristocracy or successful survivors of the fierce competition of New York City. Brilliant in technique, immensely readable and amusing, subtle and penetrating interpretations of the manners and morals of contemporary American society, Mr. Marquand's novels comprise an impressive body of work as certain of enduring life as books can be.

It is interesting to note that Mr. Marquand wrote his fine novels only after he had served a long apprenticeship writing popular romances and spy stories for the slick magazines. At one time his publishers were even hailing him with pride as "the Oppenheim of the Far East" in tribute to his tales of Oriental intrigue. The first sign of his metamorphosis into the Marquand we know today was the appearance of *Haven's End,* a collection of short stories about his home town, Newburyport, Massachusetts, which revealed his concern with the social structure of the town, with class distinctions and caste traditions.

The best way to read a Marquand novel is to plunge headlong into its delights and there relax and enjoy yourself in the company of the most thoughtfully comic writer of our time. Admire the shrewd thrusts of satiric wit; relish the joys of recognition, for you are sure to know some of the people yourself; follow the story to see what will happen, for the story is sure to be a good one most artfully told; be grateful for the fact that Mr. Marquand respects his readers' intelligence but does not consider it beneath his dignity to do his best to arouse their interest. And then, after you have had so much more than your money's worth and have read the last crisp page—then it is time enough to ponder on what it all means. You will find it means a lot.

There are layers and layers in a Marquand novel, as in an onion. After you peel back the narrative you find the social reporting: the suggestive use of all the details and apparatus of modern living, the capture for all time of the fleeting atmosphere of a period even down to the currently popular catchwords and fashionable clichés, the insight into the importance of men's public lives as well as their private characters. Private character is the customary theme of fiction, its emotional, personal, intellectual problems. Public life, which is equally important to most of us, has interested most novelists less. Its concern is with jobs, careers, money, social status, competition, etc.

And then below the social-reporting level is Mr. Marquand's satirical criticism of modern life. This can be almost as analytical as it is satiric, for Mr. Marquand is fascinated by the mechanics of society, the origin and strength of social pressures and taboos. Mr. Marquand's satire cuts a wide swath: ineffectual individuals, typical specimens of human fauna, occupational groups, foolish fashions in speech and thought, the basic assumptions of modern society.

Whereas Sinclair Lewis demolished the objects of his satire with furious frontal assaults, Mr. Marquand is content to mock them more neatly, more gently, more urbanely. His picture of life in America may not be more poetically true than that of Lewis in his best books; but it is more factually true, for it depends on much less exaggeration. And Mr. Marquand's satire is not just an objective criticism of American society; it seems to be the expression of Mr. Marquand's own deep spiritual unrest. He is a man of humor; but he is an unhappy man afflicted with all the frustrations and sense of futility, all the feeling of being alone and afraid in a world he never made, which bear so heavily upon modern men.

John Marquand's novels, taken as a whole, contain a penetrating and amazingly comprehensive panorama of American upper-class life in the twentieth century. One hundred years hence readers will be able to turn to them with absolute confidence that this was indeed the way we lived in the perplexed thirties and furious forties, that this is the way we talked, thought and felt. As accurate a reflector of his times as Anthony Trollope was of his, Mr. Marquand, being a citizen of a neurotic and anxious age instead of a confident one, is far more critical in tone than was the great Victorian.

But in our admiration for Mr. Marquand's accomplishment as a social critic and social reporter we should not lose sight of his mastery of the novel as a literary form. The skill with which he uses dialogue, time shifts and flashbacks, major crises and minor anecdotes, is breath-taking. He maintains a sustained narrative drive with almost lordly ease. And with equal dexterity he creates full-length and unforgettable characters and equally unforgettable caricatures.

George Apley is the perfect Proper Bostonian for time and eternity. H. M. Pulham, hero of the 1941 novel named after him, is a triumphant portrait of a likable, honest, decent man forced step by step to become a timid stuffed shirt by the pressures of an exclusive school, Harvard, family and Boston social traditions. But Pulham is not so exclusively a Bostonian

that there isn't something universal about him. His local proto-
types abound wherever a group of families united in "Society"
has been prosperous for three generations or more. Charles
Gray, hero of *Point of No Return,* is also much more than just
himself; he is every intelligent, ambitious young man from the
wrong side of the tracks who wins success in New York at much
cost in inner struggle and painful social adjustment.

John Marquand writes of these and his other heroes with
affectionate understanding as well as with satirical doubts.
But some of his minor characters he has torn limb from limb
with sardonic relish. Who will ever forget Bo-jo Brown, the
football hero and perpetual undergraduate of *H. M. Pulham,
Esquire?* Or Walter Newcombe, the foreign correspondent in
So Little Time, darling of the women's clubs, author of *World
Assignment,* pathetic, bumbling fool who knew that he was a
fool? Or Tom Brett, the New Deal brain truster of *B. F.'s
Daughter,* the implementer of directives and writer of speeches,
who always knew the right people, whose idealism was indistinguishable from his egotism, who felt "that manners indicated
a mental and personal vacuum?"

In writing of the feverish haste, the social pressures and the
ethical and philosophical chaos of our time John Marquand
has not always maintained an even satirical temperature. It
rises sharply in the presence of certain phenomena which pro-
voke his irritation or his wrath. It sinks to nearly normal when
he likes a character more than he dislikes him. He reached his
peak of sour disillusionment in *So Little Time.*

John Marquand does not wear his heart on his fictional
sleeve, does not reveal his private philosophy or display his
emotional troubles. But in one of his novels there is a key
which may unlock the door to his personal credo. In *B. F.'s*

Daughter one of the major characters is a corporation lawyer named Bob Tasmin. Bob was a child of privilege and conservative tradition; but he was a gentleman who lived by the finest standards of that old-fashioned concept, "gentleman," with honor and decency and kindness and intelligence. Mr. Marquand admires Bob very much, which is significant because Bob is a positive product of the same negative, petrified world as H. M. Pulham and George Apley.

Mr. Marquand seems to suggest that part of our social strife and personal unbalance is caused by the lack of a universal faith acknowledged by all subdivisions of society. And that until such a faith is found again the gentlemanly code of Bob Tasmin is a lot better than nothing.

Since satire is essentially comic and critical, satirical novels cannot be emotionally powerful. Other modern novelists have written more moving books than Mr. Marquand's, novels of nobler feeling and greater intensity. But one of the proper criteria for estimating an author's stature is productivity. Has he written more than one fine book? Has he written many? John Marquand passes this test of volume better than any other contemporary American novelist. In the last fifteen years he has written eight fine novels.

They are:

The Late George Apley, an ironic masterpiece about an elderly Boston Brahmin half petrified by the outworn codes and taboos of his caste.

Wickford Point, about the futile rebellion of younger members of the same society.

H. M. Pulham, Esquire, which has already been identified.

So Little Time, about an unhappy and self-doubting playwright and the intellectual and moral confusion which prevailed just prior to Pearl Harbor.

Repent in Haste, a novelette about a typical young pilot who fought in the Pacific and the mysterious abyss which always separates one generation from another.

B. F.'s Daughter, about marriage and morals and politics and the home front in America in wartime.

Point of No Return, about the importance of money, success and the social environment which helps to shape character and ideas during childhood and youth.

Melville Goodwin, USA, about an American general and the military mind.

Because of the remarkable homogeneity of Mr. Marquand's novels in subject matter and point of view, it has seemed best to discuss them as a whole rather than to take them up separately in detail. In one respect they are rather like Scotch whiskies. Some people don't care for them. Those who do find them all good, but some (according to taste) better than others.

XII

TWO MODERN MASTERS:

Cozzens, Cary

"It is possible to face life at its most baffling and imperfect and unideal, and yet to find it inextinguishably enthralling and splendid."—*Lord David Cecil*

Several years ago I went to lunch in the cafeteria of the *New York Times* and took with me a copy of a current novel I was reading in the line of duty. No sooner had I got well settled, with the book propped against an ash tray and a paper and pencil handy beside my fish cakes and spaghetti with tomato sauce, than a fellow employee plunked himself down across from me and fixed me with a glassy stare. "So," he said, "you're wasting your time on another novel."

"Waste?" I replied with just that shade of hauteur which the occasion seemed to demand.

"Yes," he said. "I said waste. Why don't we have any good novels about modern American life as it really is?"

"What do you mean?" I asked, sparring for time.

"I mean," he said, "that the best recent fiction has been out of touch with this country, the U.S.A. What are the outstanding novels apt to be about? I'll tell you. They're apt to be about special subjects, tiny segments of life. Childhood, madness, literary people, family life as lived in a particular locality in the past and as seen by a sensitive adolescent or an intellectual woman. The trouble with authors is that they're authors and frequently they're women. They ought to be farmers or machinists or lawyers or engineers or sales managers. Business is the most important and representative American activity, and how often does an author know anything about it?"

"I can think of some authors who are farmers and lawyers and even bankers," I said. "And given time for research I might even dig up a literary machinist or sales manager. But there's something in what you say. Most of our good writers are writers because they didn't want to be businessmen; they wanted to write. With such an abnormal urge they probably wouldn't make good businessmen anyway. But it is quite true that there are a hundred novels about love, sacred or profane, for every one which seriously explores that other subject which interests most men (if not most women) at least as much, earning a living. Something ought to be done about it."

My friend wasn't perceptibly mollified. I went on to praise the merits of fine novels which weren't about business and he did not even pretend to be interested. When he left me shortly thereafter I did not return to my book. I began to think about fiction and breadwinning. Farmers have not really been done justice in "epics of the soil," or in tales of the Deep South, which usually treat them in their nonworking hours when they have time to attend a lynching or to get on with their private experiments in miscegenation. Various businesses and professions have been satirized by Sinclair Lewis and in the New York novels. But most businessmen in fiction do not appear as such. They are more likely to be the fathers against whom their sons and daughters revolt, or strange characters venturing into an unfamiliar social world, as in the novels of Henry James or William Dean Howells.

Here, then, was a field which novelists were neglecting, the whole breadwinning aspect of life, the routine, the problems, the competition, the clash of personalities, the daily crises of men at work. John P. Marquand had touched on it brilliantly, but only as part of his larger whole, his satirical picture of modern society. Wasn't there anybody else? And then I remembered James Gould Cozzens and was astounded that I hadn't thought of him at once. His pre-eminence in this very kind of writing is unquestioned. Mr. Cozzens, even though he did receive a Pulitzer Prize for his last novel, has not yet aroused the critical enthusiasm which he deserves. And the same train of thought (writers who appreciate the importance of working hours, and writers not yet appreciated at their true worth) brought me to Joyce Cary. Both men are major novelists; both are masterly literary craftsmen.

James Gould Cozzens is the author of eleven novels, of which the first was published in 1924 when its author was a precociously gifted Harvard sophomore of twenty-one. Intoxicated by such a heady ascent to youthful glory, young Mr. Cozzens quitted college without graduating and plunged into authorship, producing several more novels in rapid succession. But it wasn't until the publication of his fifth, *S. S. San Pedro,* a brilliant story of disaster at sea, that Mr. Cozzens revealed what he could do. Three more novels followed in the 1930s and three more in the 1940s. Of these six novels four provide the grounds for my conviction that Mr. Cozzens is one of the most distinguished living American writers.

And they show in a wonderfully interesting way Mr. Cozzens' own intellectual growth. From his first book he has always been an enormously clever writer, sometimes a too clever one. His technical facility, irony, wit and cruelly analytic characterizations seemed the products of a cold-blooded craftsmanship immune to feeling. Mr. Cozzens seemed to look down on his characters from some Olympian height, understanding all, but not forgiving all, because the frailties of mortals are so stupid and so fatuous. This kind of youthful arrogance is nowhere apparent in Mr. Cozzens' best books. In *The Last Adam* and *Men and Brethren,* his two fine novels of the 1930s, it is replaced by an objectivity which may seem cold, but which never condescends and which is not indifferent to human sorrow and suffering. In *The Just and the Unjust* and *Guard of Honor,* his two superb novels of the 1940s, Mr. Cozzens' objective awareness of human failings is tempered by true compassion and a sort of stoic wisdom.

These attitudes toward his characters make the novels of James Gould Cozzens intellectually stimulating and intensely interesting. But they do insure that their appeal is primarily to the mind. One can be wholly absorbed in his fiction, filled with admiration and even awe, without being emotionally involved. One becomes extremely interested in his characters without caring much about their affairs. And it is this cool, detached quality of Mr. Cozzens' work, which, I believe, explains its lack of a large popular following. Most novels are read by women and most women who read novels demand a warmer atmosphere. They read to stir up an emotional reaction. If one is not forthcoming they don't like the book, no matter how obvious its merits.

Each of Mr. Cozzens' four major novels is devoted to a particular occupation in modern American life: *The Last Adam* to medicine, *Men and Brethren* to the ministry, *The Just and the*

Unjust to the law, and *Guard of Honor* to the army air force. Each represents several years of diligent study by its author. Mr. Cozzens can be counted on to know what he is talking about. He doesn't just collect a few superficial facts; he plunges into a special milieu and absorbs its intellectual and emotional atmosphere as well as its facts and routine. For *The Just and the Unjust* he spent years in law offices and law courts. *Guard of Honor* sprang from his own service as a major in the air corps.

But Mr. Cozzens' novels are not focused narrowly on a particular walk of life. They all range far beyond their protagonists' occupations so that they are remarkably penetrating interpretations of the general community life of which the special field of work is only a part. And they all are superb demonstrations of the crossruff between individual character and environment. Other writers have stressed social environment as a whole, in the slums or in the country-club set. But Mr. Cozzens alone among our first-class talents seems to recognize how large a part of an individual's environment consists of his occupation. By experience and inclination he is undoubtedly the best-qualified author in America to write that fine novel about an American businessman which nobody has yet written. If he only would!

The Last Adam and *Men and Brethren* are both such brilliant technical tours de force that they leave one almost gasping. For sheer human vitality, for almost inhuman knowledge of the fallible character of men and women, for technical virtuosity in the art of fiction, they are altogether astonishing. Both are short. Both are divided into many short scenes. Both demonstrate their points in wonderfully vigorous dialogue. And neither contains a likable character who can arouse sympathetic concern or personal identification. We can sympathize with their characters intellectually, because they are so intensely human and nothing human should be alien to us. But it requires an effort.

The Last Adam is the story of an elderly country doctor, a salty, courageous, stubbornly independent, moderately lazy and not very efficient doctor. It is also the story of a Connecticut village in the depression: its politics, its class distinctions, the routine of its living. It is filled with examples of Mr. Cozzens' coldly objective comments on modern life.

"Doubtless luck is the chief factor, but dispassionately considered, almost every financially unlucky person is a plain fool to start with."

"Dispassionately considered"—these words may well be the key to the world of James Gould Cozzens. He considers the world dispassionately, never laments the times and seasons, throws a bright light on human beings as they are without denouncing them, or the gods, because they are not different, or because life includes war as well as peace, suffering and disaster as well as happiness and tranquillity.

The hero of *Men and Brethren,* the Reverend Ernest Cudlip, is a Protestant Episcopal clergyman, a sophisticated, witty, cultivated man fond of music, wine and French cooking; a mildly arrogant man with few amiable weaknesses who yet is sincerely devout, extremely generous and fundamentally good. Mr. Cozzens' novel covers only two days in Ernest Cudlip's life, hectic days in which a half-dozen people pestered him for help in the messy and desperately human problems in which they had entangled themselves through sin and folly.

Men and Brethren is a revealing look at weak and erring humanity through the eyes of orthodox Christian faith. How much Mr. Cozzens shares Cudlip's theology and philosophy, or whether he shares them at all, cannot be told from his book. But it is illuminating to look at lechery and concupiscence, false pride and cheap self-interest, through Cudlip's eyes. Cudlip's worldly knowledge of the unmoral and amoral modern world in no way lessened his devotion to another world, the world of Christian faith and charity, and of practical good works in the tradition of the good Samaritan.

With *The Just and the Unjust* Mr. Cozzens broadened the range of his fiction, softened the sharp edge of his dispassionate consideration with more readily noticed compassion and probed more deeply into American life. *The Just and the Unjust* is a novel about the law and the actual way in which freedom under law operates in our American democracy. It is a demonstration and a consideration of the letter and spirit, the theory and practice of law. Its deep immersion in the technical lore of a difficult subject in no way hampers its effectiveness as an engrossing story.

Structurally, this is the story of a murder trial. The defendants are three smalltime criminals who killed a man in the course of a clumsy kidnaping. The characters are the prosecuting attorneys, defense lawyers, judges, witnesses; their friends, relatives, political and social connections. The trial moves forward slowly and inexorably, dramatically unfolding the character of everyone associated with it. As each witness contributes his bit another human being is revealed; and the tricks and mechanics of legal procedure, cross-examination, appeal to the jury and deference to the judge are all made clear and dramatic. But *The Just and the Unjust* is not confined to the courtroom and one case.

Its hero, Abner Coates, assistant district attorney, an able but stuffy and commonplace man, is in love in his spare time, and he is concerned in a number of other cases, each of which illuminates another aspect of the law: a disputed will, an automobile accident, a nasty scandal over a teacher's betrayal of trust in the local high school.

Mr. Cozzens goes behind the scenes after court adjourns and shows the lawyers for the opposing sides fraternizing, joking, bickering and wrangling in the lawyers' room. He shows the influence and power of the county political boss, who can win for Abner the nomination for district attorney, and Abner's distaste for catering to him.

There are three judges in this story, one of them Abner's invalid father, and each, although properly reflecting his own personality, has something significant to say about the law or human nature.

"Don't be cynical," Judge Coates says. "A cynic is just a man who found out when he was about ten that there wasn't any Santa Claus, and he's still upset. Yes, there'll be more wars; and soon, I don't doubt. There always have been. There'll be deaths and disappointments and failures. When they come, you meet them. Nobody promises you a good time or an easy time. I don't know who it was who said when we think of the past we regret and when we think of the future we fear. And with reason. But no bets are off. There is the present to think of, and as long as you live there always will be. In the present, every day is a miracle. The world gets up in the morning and is fed and goes to work, and in the evening it comes home and is fed again and perhaps has a little amusement and goes to sleep. To make that possible, so much has to be done by so many people that, on the face of it, it is impossible. Well, every day we do it; and every day, come hell, come high water, we're going to have to go on doing it as well as we can."

Judge Coates or James Gould Cozzens speaking, it makes small difference. It is a sound and coolly intelligent thought for the day in these tumultuous times.

There is much that is brilliant in *The Just and the Unjust,* much that is wise, much that is an important reflection of modern America. There are flashes of insight in these pages so sharp and true that they are apt to stir the reader to appreciative response. "Why, yes," one is frequently prompted to exclaim, "that's exactly right, only I could never put it (if I could think it) half so well myself!"

There are a balance, a restraint, a wholeness of viewpoint, a human inclusiveness in *The Just and the Unjust* which are altogether admirable. Mr. Cozzens does not fail to show that men can be petty, mean, stupid, selfish, cruel and foulmouthed; but he also shows that they can be rocklike in their integrity, patient, just and tolerant. *The Just and the Unjust* concerns a murder trial and in its slow-moving fashion builds up considerable suspense as to the verdict; it concerns the law and does not indulge in cheap cries of "woe unto you lawyers"; it concerns a small American town. But out of all these matters it fuses a fine novel about very human beings and the stuff of democracy itself.

Equally impressive in its understanding of all sorts and conditions of men and equally expert in its technical craftsmanship is *Guard of Honor.* This panoramic novel of life in a great air-force base in Florida during only three days is not primarily a war novel, although it deals with a military organization in wartime. It is a novel about two kinds of Americans: career members of the air force whose ideas, patterns of thought and outlook on life have been molded by life in it, and civilians adapting themselves to the strange new environment of a military organization.

Like Mr. Cozzens' other books, *Guard of Honor* is divided into many short scenes filled with the clash of personalities and alive with vibrant and revealing dialogue. But it is told from the points of view of a wider assortment of characters. Of these two are the most important. They are Captain Nathaniel Hicks, thirty-eight years old, a successful magazine editor in civilian life, and Colonel Norman Ross, in his late fifties, a lawyer and a judge.

With extraordinary skill Mr. Cozzens has twined together a variety of different problems and combustible situations into one unified whole. One of these is a potentially explosive race conflict involving a unit of colored officers. Another is the psychological problem of Major General Ira N. ("Bus") Beal, the youngest two-star general in the air force. Beal was a great airman and fighter pilot, a fine leader of men and a brave man, but a simple, forthright, impulsive soul. Did he have the tact, the patience, the diplomatic astuteness to be a successful executive? Could Colonel Ross with his subtler mind and greater maturity of judgment guide him through the shoals of military politics? Another is the relationship of Captain Hicks, a good man too far away from his wife and children, and an appealing WAC lieutenant.

It would be hard to think of any novel in modern fiction in which so many different characters are brought to such triumphant life. With sympathetic understanding, with occasional flashes of satire, with wonderful dexterity, Mr. Cozzens has moved them from space to space on his complicated chessboard, never losing sight of his central narrative, making the bewilder-

[189]

ing variety of technical air operations clear and interesting in the process. He does not overlook red tape, military rituals and the presence of square pegs in round holes; but neither does he overlook the great achievements which the air force accomplished in a hurry.

And *Guard of Honor* is distinguished by the same shafts of insight, the same cool, detached wisdom that illuminated *The Just and the Unjust*. Here is Colonel Ross brooding on the case of General Beal:

"Not that General Beal lacked, or would imagine he lacked, unusual abilities which he could use—had used—with confidence; but he might feel that he owed his chances to use them to something outside, rather than something inside, himself. Colonel Ross must admit that modesty of this kind was pleasing in a man who had risen to high place; yet it was not (perhaps unfortunately for the world) the basic stuff of greatness. It spoke a simplicity of nature little related to the complexities, often unpleasant, of those natures that are resolved to lead, and also, by a suggestion of mystery and power in those very complexities, apt to impose leadership—the able, queer, vain men who in large-scale emergencies are turned to, and so make history. . . . Anyone was lucky who could go a successful way without the call to exercise greatness, without developing greatness's enabling provisions—the great man's inner contradictions; his mean, inspired inconsistencies; his giddy acting on hunches; and his helpless, not mere modest acceptance of, but passionate, necessary trust in, luck."

James Gould Cozzens' flair for characterization, his understanding of individual Americans and the American scene in general, his interest in men working and his dispassionate consideration of life are all so notable that in discussing his work there is a danger of underestimating his professional skill as a novelist. His technical competence is extraordinarily high. He always knows just what effects he wishes to obtain and obtains them perfectly. He is a master of dialogue, of interior monologues, of flashbacks, of narrative pace and selective form. His style is precise and smooth, graceful and unobtrusive, always so subordinated to the matter of his novels that it is hardly noticeable at all. Avoiding the more topical and ephemeral issues of our time, keeping his personal views on the crisis of modern man to himself, severely eliminating any trace of his own emotions, Mr. Cozzens lets his fiction speak for itself. It does so with such an authentic ring of truth, with such firm and quiet eloquence, that James Gould Cozzens' rank among the foremost American novelists of his generation seems beyond dispute.

Although there are striking resemblances between the novels of James Gould Cozzens and those of Joyce Cary, there are almost equally striking differences. Both men are literary virtuosos of formidable skill. Both are awesomely knowing about human character and profound students of human society. Both are fascinated and excited by the wonderful drama of human life. Both write objectively, without indulging personal mannerisms or defending private opinions.

But Arthur Joyce Lunel Cary, Irish-born English poet, political scientist and novelist, is a flashier, more exuberant writer. His delight in people, in storytelling and in the various techniques he employs with bravura skill enriches his work with a breathless enthusiasm for life and art which is contagious.

As each of Mr. Cary's novels appears in this country it becomes increasingly apparent that Joyce Cary is one of the most gifted of practicing English novelists. He is equally adept in a variety of fictional techniques. There are few walks of life, few classes of society, few occupations, about which he cannot write with complete authority. His insight into the inmost depths of human beings is profound. His understanding of the social changes which have transformed the world in the last half century is impressive. A novelist who never fails to tell a rousing story, he writes with a gusto and sense of the excitement and drama of life which are rare indeed in this age of mincing talents and literary pretensions. Mr. Cary's inexhaustible imagination and comic zest stem from the great tradition of Dickens and Fielding. To touch one of his books is to touch something alive.

Joyce Cary was born December 7, 1888. He studied at Trinity College, Dublin, and at Oxford and went off to the Balkan War in 1912 because he wanted to get a look at what he thought might be the last war in his lifetime. For seven years from 1913 through 1920 he served in the colonial service in Nigeria, including a session fighting the Germans in the Cameroons in the First World War. He has studied painting and is an ardent amateur painter. His first novel was not published until 1932 when he was forty-three. He has written twelve. Of these one was published in this country in the 1930s. Six more were brought out here between 1947 and 1951. They provide a portrait gallery of some of the most vital, comic, raffish, representative and unforgettable characters in modern fiction.

Mister Johnson, the earliest of the six in the order of their original composition, was the last to be published in the United States. This strange and brilliant book is a breath-taking full-length characterization of an extraordinary human being. It is also a colorful and dramatic story filled with shafts of sardonic satire and outbursts of primitive poetry. Drawing on his personal experience of the Nigerian bush country, Mr. Cary has written the comic, pitiful, nearly tragic story of a young native clerk working for the government in the jungle town of Fada, the capital of a native emirate.

Mr. Johnson had learned to read and write English at a mission school, but he had not learned the value of money or even how to add a few figures together correctly. It was money and Mr. Johnson's imagination which brought about his downfall. Although Mr. Cary has laced his pages with suggestive details of the Nigerian scene, neatly impaled several footling and feckless white characters and acidly lampooned the British colonial service, Johnson dwarfs everything else in the book named after him as completely as did George F. Babbitt in the book named after him.

Johnson was a Christian and a "government man," civilized and scornful of bush people and pagans. But his mind was more in tune with the bush than with the inexplicable taboos of civilization; Johnson was in reality a bewildered child lost between two worlds. Emotional and demonstrative, soaring from tearful lamentations to paroxysms of lyrical joy, Johnson lived in the present and let his imagination rule his life.

Kind, sentimental, gregarious, infantilely vain, Johnson craved the admiration of others and the approval of his own ego. So he lied and boasted and got drunk and piled up debts and bilked his creditors and stole money for the best of reasons: to make himself important and admired, to please his wife, to entertain his friends, to get himself out of a fix. Johnson did not mean to do wrong; he just couldn't recognize the existence of the obligations and responsibilities of the white man's world. He was a criminal, but he committed his worst crimes in a spirit of primeval innocence.

Mr. Johnson is strange and pitiful and a little more than

[193]

life-size. Mr. Cary likes him, is amused by him and pities him; but he never condescends to him. Poor Johnson's story is funny and pathetic and rich with ironic implications about morality, sociology and empire.

But so are all Mr. Cary's novels rich with unstated implications. His relish in the humanness of men and women is equaled only by his fascination in their moral codes, their social customs, the continual revolutions which are always transforming their society. He never explains or expounds these matters. He suggests with a glancing word and demonstrates in action, and the reader may draw his own conclusions. He can draw any number from the three novels which comprise the trilogy which is Mr. Cary's best-known work.

Loosely linked together by the fact that the central character in each is a minor character in the other two, these novels are *Herself Surprised, To Be a Pilgrim* and *The Horse's Mouth*. All three are absolute triumphs of wit and blazingly brilliant characterization; but the first is the simplest and most warmly appealing of Mr. Cary's books and the last is the most peculiar and difficult.

Herself Surprised is as warm in its general tone as the heart of its heroine, as surprising, engaging, paradoxical, wise and foolish a woman as ever failed to distinguish the difference between virtue and sin. Sara Monday tells her own story in the first person with a mixture of naïveté and innate shrewdness which is remarkably authentic. Her language, her philosophy and her habits are all naturally and perfectly right. It seems impossible that a mere man could have written *Herself Surprised,* or that any woman except Sara could have written it either.

This is the tart, amusing, fast-moving story of a woman who came into conflict with society and the law because of her inability to refrain from trying to make weak men happy. There were three men in Sara's life and the only one she really loved and wanted to protect didn't love her or want to be protected. Sara frankly recognized her "nature," as she called it, and men's nature, and granted her favors gladly. She was a little careless about money, too, and other people's property; but her intentions were entirely innocent. There was never a less criminally minded woman than Sara. In fact, few women have been so sensible, so kind, so generous and so utterly. without envy or meanness. Sara wouldn't have had any trouble at all, really, if her men had only been halfway decent instead of such a moldy lot.

Herself Surprised is a comic gem, a high-spirited frolic which sports with conventional ideas of character, love and morality. Far more serious in atmosphere and subject matter is its successor, *To Be a Pilgrim*. Although it, too, is a personal confession told in the first person without a false note, *To Be a Pilgrim* is also a study of intellectual, moral, social and political change.

Thomas Wilcher, elderly bachelor not always quite right in his head, was a lawyer, a churchwarden and an aristocrat, and also a man who sometimes got into trouble with the police because of his weakness for forcing his attentions upon young women in public parks. He does not write in Sara's simple, racy fashion. His prose is tightly woven, compressed, packed with ideas, memories and sad reflections. It requires close attention and rewards it.

With slippery grace Mr. Wilcher's attention continually slips from the present to the past. He lives in two worlds—the today in which he is a sick old man with an uncertain mind, and the long yesterday of his memories of childhood, family life, love, politics and the erstwhile strength of the Protestant religious

[195]

tradition in English life. Mr. Wilcher's mercurial memories break his story into many short scenes, each composed largely in dialogue.

Many characters are thus introduced and all of them have an extraordinary vitality. But interesting and dramatic as they are, they are dwarfed by Mr. Wilcher himself, one of the most subtly developed, complete and original characters in modern fiction. A foolish, futile and weak eccentric, Mr. Wilcher is crotchety, irascible and sometimes mad. But he is also intelligent, sensitive and understanding of others. His love for England, for traditional standards, for beauty and for his family is strong and fine. His religious faith is sincere and important to him. Contemplating the strange new world of the twenties and thirties with their fetish of materialism he is acutely unhappy, not just as an old man mourning his youth, but as an intelligent man aware of the sad state of the modern world. Thomas Wilcher's weaknesses are deplorable, but he has an integrity of his own.

And this quality of integrity of character, of being true to oneself, crops up in many of Mr. Cary's novels. It is one of the principal themes of *The Horse's Mouth,* the astounding self-revelation of an amoral ruffian who happened to be an artist of genius. Gulley Jimson, who hadn't been a gentleman for forty years, takes up his story at the age of sixty-seven when he has just been released from jail.

It is a dramatic story; several of its episodes are hilariously comic. It is imaginatively inventive, fairly bouncing with vigor and unquenchable delight in raffish people, alive with Bohemian madness. But *The Horse's Mouth* is much more than this; Gulley's seemingly artless chatter is the most convincing presentation of artistic genius I have ever encountered in print. It is an intellectually exciting adventure to look at life and art through the distorted vision of Gulley Jimson.

It is not easy at first. Gulley writes as he thinks, in images of color and design, with exuberant richness of metaphor and alarming figures of speech. He cannot look at anything without thinking of pictures, patterns and colors. His passion for imaginative creation is a fierce joy to him. If he can't paint he can think about painting. He doesn't give a hoot for security, society, respectability, custom or law. Gulley is an old rascal; but he is a gallant one with a private philosophy of his own. His story is ablaze with nonsense and beauty, with fun and wisdom all served up with such devilish skill that *The Horse's Mouth* is Mr. Cary's most glittering performance.

The fact that Thomas Wilcher and Gulley Jimson are two of Sara Monday's men is not of much significance in tying Mr. Cary's trilogy together. Three more disparate characters would be hard to imagine, or three novels more different in spirit. But they are linked together by one quality which they have in common: all three concern characters who are outcasts from society. Mr. Cary never strays far from his preoccupation with the way the world goes, what men and women do in it, and the shifting codes and conventions which they either accept or defy. His two most recent novels are less devoted to one dominating character and so are all the more closely focused on this theme.

The Moonlight is technically expert and intellectually interesting, as all Mr. Cary's novels are. Its dramatization of moral codes and the way thinking about love and sex has changed between the end of the last century and the middle of this one is impressively done. But it is a colder, more detached and objective book than its predecessors. None of its half-dozen major

[197]

characters is appealing or sympathetic, although all of them are intensely real. Mr. Cary has never faltered for a moment in any of his novels in either the high quality of his characterization or in the deft and logical construction of his story. *The Moonlight* is a masterly novel which compels admiration; but it is more sober, less original in theme and lacking in the infectious zest for living which is present in all Mr. Cary's other books.

Joyce Cary's last novel, *A Fearful Joy,* was written under difficulties during a time of emotional tension and personal loss. It is the weakest of his novels. But it, too, is brilliant. Mr. Cary doesn't write novels which aren't brilliant. Its panorama of English society from the 1890s to the present is vigorous and amusing, crammed with satirical and comic impressions of typical groups, follies, fads, behavior patterns—from the poets and aesthetes of the nineties to the tough, disillusioned and courageously irresponsible postwar young people of today. Its many characters are as solid and real and lively as Mr. Cary's characters always are.

But the reason *A Fearful Joy* falters is that its two magnificently drawn major characters are not interesting. They are alive and believable and representative; but they are tiresome. No matter how vital, swaggering, lusty and comic *A Fearful Joy* is, and it is all those things, no matter how amusing are several of its episodes, and they are very amusing, it is difficult to stir up much concern over its story of a competent and commonplace woman who took a fearful joy in her love for a worthless man.

But it is interesting to note that *A Fearful Joy* does not seem quite so objective in its point of view as *The Moonlight* or *To Be a Pilgrim,* Mr. Cary's other two novels most concerned with social change. Joyce Cary is not charmed by the self-interest and self-indulgence of modern society, by the refusal of many people to recognize moral obligations. Without indulging in moralizing he looks on such aberrations in *A Fearful Joy* with an air of stoic resignation. After all, no novelist as shrewd as Joyce Cary, except James Gould Cozzens, can study the modern world and remain completely objective. It is remarkable enough that Mr. Cary has kept his own reactions to himself as much as he has.

XIII

Godden, Winslow, Wickenden

"With each new happening, perhaps with each person
we meet if they are important to us, we must either be
born again, or die a little bit; big deaths and little ones,
big and little births."
—*Captain John in* The River *by Rumer Godden*

One of the delights of fiction is its infinite variety. No one
need fast where such an ample feast is spread. There is a dish
for every taste. Those who care to can sup on horrors; but those
who long since were surfeited with such strong meat can dine
on more delicate fare.

Contemporary novelists are all citizens of the same unhappy
world. When the winds of wrath blow up a tempest in Korea,
Cambodia, Iran or the Potsdamer Platz they all shiver with
equal apprehension. Whatever their nationality, their philosophy or their metabolism, they walk in the dark beside the same
haunted graveyard. Some try to exercise their fears with shouts
of fierce defiance. Some, and they are a select and superior company, choose to speak in a quiet voice about less horrendous
matters, the timeless truths of character and experience which
are always the same, yesterday, today and tomorrow.

The Essence of Experience

This is not a literary "escape" (oh much abused word!), but a fitting and proper example of the shoemaker sticking to his last. Topical problems can blacken the sun and convulse civilization. But everyone cannot say something useful or important about them. And topical problems are like an interminable parade. The parade never passes, but every time you look away for a moment a different band is playing a different tune. In the long perspective of literary history nothing is more ephemeral than a burning issue. Works of fiction do not survive because they dramatize the debate over Chartism or the menace to a sound currency in the free coinage of silver. They endure past their own time because they contain truths which are equally true in any time.

If a novelist opposes tyranny and slavery, fascism and communism, why, that is what he must do. He can do no less and remain an honest man. If he can warn his contemporaries of their horrors with the cogency and eloquence of an Orwell or a Koestler, he has struck a shrewd blow on the side of the angels. But his is a political and topical achievement. The novelist's success as a writer is always judged in the long run by his skill in creating characters, telling stories and interpreting life according to his private vision of it.

A few writers can persuade their readers that they have cast a ray of light into the secret places of the heart, that they have increased by a mite the sum of human understanding about life and love and death, grief and loneliness and the misery of growing up. Theirs is no mean feat. It is a high art to distill the essence of experience into fiction. And to do so without adding to the general din, in a quiet voice, with taste, simplicity and sure technical craftsmanship, is to contribute something rare and fine to a world sadly in need of it. Three modern novelists who have done just this in unobtrusive ways distinctively their own are Rumer Godden, Anne Goodwin Winslow and Dan Wickenden.

Rumer Godden is an English woman who spent her childhood in India and who has lived much of her life abroad. She is the author of seven novels, a collection of personal notes about life on a tea plantation high in the Himalayas, a long poem and several books for children. She is a fine artist, one of the most accomplished of living English novelists.

Of Miss Godden's seven novels only one, *Gypsy, Gypsy,* is unsuccessful and only one other, her last, *A Breath of Air,* falls somewhat below her extraordinarily high standard, although it, too, has lovely qualities. The remaining five are all splendid, triumphs of precise and subtle craftsmanship, exquisitely, delicately, almost austerely written, serenely wise and deeply moving, witty and compassionate. They are: *Black Narcissus, Breakfast with the Nikolides, Take Three Tenses, The River* and *A Candle for St. Jude.* Few currently productive writers can rival such a list.

All of Rumer Godden's novels, although their themes and backgrounds vary widely, are primarily concerned with the mysteries of human character and personality, the development of individuals. Equally adroit at portraying old age or childhood, she reveals her characters in speech and thought and action and wastes little space in writing *about* them. Her prose is so pure, limpid and deceptively simple that it often conceals the finished artistry and complicated methods of her storytelling. So deft are her shifts of time sequences and so expert her use of little dabs of stream-of-consciousness writing that these devices never cause a ripple in the smooth current of her novels.

As all really distinguished writers do, Rumer Godden stamps

every page she writes with the imprint of her personality and the special quality of her vision of life. And she does so without distorting her novels into mere media for the expression of her personal social and political views. Whatever they may be, they are not to be found in her books. Instead, partly by the translucent beauty of her prose and partly by her insight into the eternal verities of human living, she impregnates her writing with a compassionate wisdom and serene understanding unique in modern fiction. Her books not only interest and amuse; they illuminate.

The world of Rumer Godden is filled with intangibles of atmosphere and personality, with nuances of character caused by place and race and the impact of people on one another. It is not a happy world, for she is too aware of the hurts and aches of living. But it is not a glum and sordid world either. There is too much love and humor in it, too much joy in beauty for that. And above all there is a calm acceptance of the double nature of life, its inextricable mixture of good and evil, of delight and misery, which reflects a serenity of spirit close to true wisdom.

Black Narcissus was published in 1939 and so falls outside the compass of this book. It is a subtle, psychologically fascinating and hauntingly beautiful novel about the efforts of a group of Anglican nuns to establish a convent in a remote valley in the Himalayas. The havoc wrought in religious bosoms by the frosty majesty of mountain splendors, the curious beliefs of dusky pupils and the disturbing presences of an Oriental prince and an alcoholic Englishman, is described with delicate irony and sincere compassion.

In *Gypsy, Gypsy* Miss Godden attempted a form of fiction for which she had no real bent—psychological melodrama. Although she conjured up some sinister excitement and managed to make a coldly evil woman believable as well as villainous, *Gypsy, Gypsy* never quite jells into a successful whole.

With *Breakfast with the Nikolides* we come to Miss Godden's personal favorite among her books, a preference she acknowledged when I told her that *The River* is my own. It is easy to see why she feels as she does, for *Breakfast with the Nikolides* is the most subtle in characterization and the most emotionally powerful of all her novels.

This is a story of many strands woven expertly into a complex whole. It is laid in Bengal, where Miss Godden herself lived as a child, and concerns the emotional crisis which beset a whole community when a neurotic and hysterical woman assumed that her daughter's spaniel had hydrophobia and sent the child and her sister to a neighbor's for breakfast so that she might have the dog killed in their absence. The consequences of this treachery changed the lives of many people: the mother's and her estranged husband's, the daughter's, that of the low-caste Hindu veterinarian who was bullied into dispatching the dog, and that of the veterinarian's best friend, an aristocratic young Indian poet.

With consummate skill Miss Godden builds up an atmosphere of oppressive tension in the midst of the more general atmosphere of India. Her characters are brilliantly revealed, Indian and English with equal understanding. And in eleven-year-old Emily, the proud, stubborn, imaginative daughter of a selfish, stupid and neurotic woman, Miss Godden is little short of triumphant. Emily's implacable will to retaliate against her mother is unforgettable. She is both a frightening and a pitiful child, and an intensely real one. *Breakfast with the Nikolides* might have been a melodrama. But because of Miss Godden's objectivity and restraint it is a tragicomedy filled with glinting humor and suggestive implications.

Take Three Tenses, Miss Godden's next novel, is an intricately constructed fantasy about a family and an old house, and about character and time. It begins with an old man brooding in lonely state, holding communion with the past and with the dead who still fill his house with their vital presences.

As he does so time itself dissolves out of its customary triple order and the three tenses, past, present and future, blend into one. As a musical fugue can keep several melodies in simultaneous flight, so Miss Godden's story juggles the past and the future and makes them both contemporary with the present. It is as if she had shredded time into gossamer threads and rewoven them into a pattern of her own.

The house contained within it all that had happened there and all that would happen. Only the right chord had to be struck to set the echoes ringing. For houses, Miss Godden seems to say, are individual entities with personalities soaked up from all the living and dying that have gone on within their walls. The idea may be fanciful, but Miss Godden makes it very real. All the meals which were served and eaten, all the mail and packages which were delivered, all the spite and grief and love and happiness of No. 99 Wiltshire Place, London, could not vanish completely.

Take Three Tenses is not only an experiment which sports with conventional conceptions of time; it is an experiment in fictional method. Miss Godden, by demolishing chronology, dispenses with the usual aids to suspense and narrative interest. You already know what happens next. By not using flashbacks, but by stirring segments of time all together, Miss Godden isn't even able to use customary storytelling devices in small bits. *Take Three Tenses* depends entirely on its ability to endow with individual interest a cavalcade of characters from four generations and to make them seem symbolical of all human living.

This it does well. There are a melancholy sort of poetry and a poignant nostalgia in its pages which cast a genuine spell. As a painting by Van Gogh doesn't really look like a wheat field in bright sunshine and yet conveys a powerful impression of just that, so *Take Three Tenses* is an eloquent impression of the sad realities of life, of the aromatic bitterness of lost love and of the joy of ever-renewing hope.

At first glance *The River* seems only a beguiling short novel about children set against the familiar Indian background Miss Godden knows so well. Even if it were only that, *The River* would still be delightful, for Miss Godden can suggest much of India with a few details and she has a wonderful way with children, tender and true and never sentimental. For sheer spell-casting charm *The River* is a flawless gem.

But the still waters of *The River* run deep. Beneath their tranquil surface lie unexpectedly rich treasures. Miss Godden's narrow focus, confined as it is to four children, a nurse and a family friend, excludes much; but like beams of light concentrated through a microscope it also reveals much that is normally hidden. A fresh look at the mysteries of life and love and individual responsibility can be vastly stimulating.

Harriet, the heroine, was about thirteen. Half of her wanted to stay a child; half wanted to grow up. Harriet wanted to know, to understand, to feel, all with a fierce intensity. She wanted to be important someday and already realized how few people were. She wanted to understand Captain John, who had lost a leg in the war, who was strong enough to bear great pain, who had strange, wise thoughts; but who, sometimes, wasn't any more knowing or certain of things than she was. There was so much war and misery in the world, and so much love still in it, too. "Funny," said Harriet to herself, "the world goes on living and it has all those troubles in it."

Harriet is one of the nicest heroines of modern fiction. She is also a fine characterization of a sensitive, idealistic, imaginative child. Such children are often pretty poisonous in literature. Harriet is the reverse, as simple and believable as she is lovable. *The River* is a deeply moving book as well as an exquisitely written one.

In *A Candle for St. Jude* Rumer Godden treats with perfection a subject which has baffled numerous other writers, the ingrown world of the ballet. Instead of the flamboyance, the hysterics and the panting amours generally considered essential, she writes about two days in the life of a small London ballet theater and school. She writes with authority; but she never allows a breath of the hothouse air or the mincing affectations of some balletomanes to infect her story.

Madame Anna Holbein, for twenty years an international star and for thirty an impresario of her own productions danced by her own pupils, is a small, tired, indomitable figure. Not strictly truthful, inclined to bully, at once gallant and pathetic, she is as passionately devoted to perfection in ballet as the most exacting traditions of that complicated art require. Madame is the only full-length character in *A Candle for St. Jude.* The others revolve around her like minor planets. She is revealed in the round, complete with her wistful memories of past glories and her sudden flashes of brutally candid self-examination.

A Candle for St. Jude in its quiet way is a witty book. Its power to evoke for a few hours the strange climate and special customs of the ballet world is uncanny. Its success in creating

[207]

one passionate, capricious, gifted and dedicated character is complete. It, too, is one of Rumer Godden's triumphs.

In her last novel, *A Breath of Air,* Miss Godden forsakes the real world for a world of dreams and tells an airy fairy story about an imaginary island, which, like all proper dream islands, is a haven of serenity and beauty. Although recurrent gleams of satire recall the real world of strife and sorrow, I imagine that Miss Godden took refuge on the languorous shores of Terraqueous in order to remove the real world for a blessed interval to a comfortable distance.

A Breath of Air is charming, but it is well below Miss Godden's miraculously high average. It depends too much on the enchantment of mere words and on the soft delights of a fancifully idyllic scene. The characters who act out this palely lovely little fable are as brightly insubstantial as butterflies. They have both wise and foolish thoughts, but they have no individual life. And, since both characters and plot of *A Breath of Air* are a modern-dress version of Shakespeare's *The Tempest,* that very fact proves intrusive and distracting.

By half closing one's eyes, by refusing to think of *A Breath of Air* as a novel, a fantasy, or as anything contrived by literary art, it is possible to float off into a sort of sleepy trance which is delightful. And every now and then one is awakened by a clear, cool, true thought, which one has probably met before, but never dressed in more becoming words.

It is easy to understand why Rumer Godden wished to relax on Terraqueous after the strain of her more subtle, intense and creative work. *A Breath of Air* is a minor effort which in no way diminishes the importance of her achievement. Her five fine novels are infused with a gentle beauty which is not only verbal but also of the mind.

The Essence of Experience

The only American writer I know of who at all resembles Rumer Godden is Anne Goodwin Winslow, who does so to a surprising degree.

Mrs. Winslow is older by a generation, a Southerner who writes most frequently of the South as she knew it in her childhood and youth in the last century. She writes fiction with the same nice precision, an equally cool and translucent prose and a similar feminine concentration on the truths of individual relationships and inner experience.

Anne Goodwin Winslow is that admirable rarity, a lady born and bred who has never had time or inclination to be just a lady. Instead she has been a far-wandering army officer's wife, a celebrated hostess, a poet, a woman of gentle wit and rueful wisdom and a novelist of enchanting charm.

All Mrs. Winslow's books are artful, calm, precise and delicate, products of sound technical skill and reflections of a distinctive personality. The silken sensibility of her reactions to life, the patient, tolerant and tranquilly reflective attitude she displays toward erring human nature and the serene grace of her quiet humor make Mrs. Winslow seem a little like a gracious guest from another, more civilized era doomed to spend a too-long protracted visit in our shrill and strident age.

Most of Mrs. Winslow's stories are laid in the South in the 1890s, during a time when the eternal problems of personal experience were just the same as always, but when they more often presented themselves clothed in seemly manners and traditional decorum. Like Willa Cather in her later years, Mrs. Winslow yearns for a past which, although it had many imperfections, had none so darkly tragic as the present's. She likes to write of ladies and gentlemen, of soft-spoken people in quiet neighborhoods, and to find meaning and significance in their

[209]

outwardly uneventful lives as important as others find in bedrooms or on barricades.

Like the true artist she is, Mrs. Winslow leaves much unsaid.
Her stories suggest, but do not underline; create a powerful
emotional impression, but do not offer pat conclusions. They
deal with a world in which intangibles of emotion, refinements
of human relationships and carefully considered attitudes toward life itself are important. But they are important only
insofar as Mrs. Winslow's characters (or her readers) can perceive them or achieve them by their own efforts without explicit
directions. As in life itself, so in her stories only those who seek
shall find.

Which isn't the same thing as saying that they are obscure or
difficult; only that they mean different things to different readers. Most of her stories are seen through the eyes of feminine
characters, and all of them seem very feminine indeed. They
do not concern the harsh necessities of breadwinning, or the
violence and degradation of life. They deal with matters which
so many women have always thought more important: love
won and lost, the infinite complexities of personal relationships,
marriage and children.

Many books compel admiration without winning affection.
Mrs. Winslow's do the reverse. Their readers (some whom I
know, anyway) become so fond of them that they sometimes
forget the many good reasons why they are admirable, as is
often the case with dear ones.

Except for a volume of verse published many years ago Anne
Goodwin Winslow has written all her books late in life, after
she became a widow and a grandmother. The first, *The Dwelling Place,* a volume of casual Southern reminiscences, appeared
in 1943. The second, *A Winter in Geneva and Other Stories,*

consists of a long novelette and six short stories. The other four are novels.

The Dwelling Place is a small and choice book. Its family stories, mellow little essays and reminiscent talk are entirely unpretentious and entirely charming. They deal with guests and ghosts, painters and peacocks, gardens and magnolias, black and white neighbors and the continuous performance of the passing seasons—and most of all with life in the old house in Raleigh, Tennessee, where they were written. The easy grace of Mrs. Winslow's meandering meditations provides a polite and formal introduction to the healthy vigor of her thought.

Mrs. Winslow's husband once said to her that she was always happy. Of course she wasn't and never expected to be. But she was always interested. What a zest and relish for life that capacity to be interested reveals! If more of us could regard the life around us with Mrs. Winslow's alert, curious and observant interest we would have less time to be unhappy.

The novelette called *A Winter in Geneva* is a fresh and highly individual reworking of an old theme, that favorite of Henry James, the education of an American woman in Europe. As James so often did, Mrs. Winslow takes for her heroine an American woman of lively intelligence and warm sympathies whose eyes have not yet been opened to the realities of evil and the disillusioned realism of ancient peoples. Elizabeth Roberts, wintering in Geneva with her little boy in 1924-25, was a very attractive and likable person. But in her fundamental innocence, her American insistence on judging all human conduct by the inflexible moral standards preached, if not always practiced, in her native Kentucky, she blundered and caused sorrow and suffering and almost tragedy. Virtue, she found, is inadequate equipment for life. Knowledge too is necessary—and sympathy and understanding of other people's misguided points of view.

Mrs. Winslow's first full-length novel, *Cloudy Trophies,* is her least successful book. Although it contains considerable beauty and stimulation to thought, it is a trifle fuzzy in motivation and rather baffling in its omission of essential information. But if she stumbles with *Cloudy Trophies,* she more than makes up for it with her next two books, which are her finest.

A Quiet Neighborhood is a story of life in a Southern village not too far from a town which might be Memphis. In Cherry Station there was a local culture, a sense of social unity and a mannered grace which were partly Southern, partly small-town and partly late nineteenth-century. Wealth had been slipping away since the War between the States; but the codes of conduct and the sense of security of a happier century than ours were still powerful influences.

There were yellow fever in Cherry Station, and murder committed by no-account Negroes, and arson and fraud committed by no-account whites. But nobody minded much and everyone was intent on maintaining pleasant personal relations. Only the conspicuously thoughtful tried to understand the philosophy of Cherry Station life, if there was one; or if there wasn't, to find one for themselves which would fit it. But it was about such thoughtful people that Mrs. Winslow writes. *A Quiet Neighborhood* is filled with good talk about ideas, with the ordinary chitchat of social intercourse held to a minimum.

Paring her story of all excess decoration and every unnecessary detail, Mrs. Winslow writes a succession of short scenes which blend imperceptibly into one another, each revealing a little more about three very nice people and the inmost recesses of their beings. The three are involved in an emotional and adequately dramatic situation. What they discover about themselves and about life is the core of *A Quiet Neighborhood.* Its gentle wisdom and crystalline prose are not commonly met with in American fiction. The only book I know of where they are equaled is Mrs. Winslow's next, *The Springs.*

The Springs is the story of Alice Macgowan's growing-up in the 1890s, how she changes in a few years from the innocence of childhood to the maturity which comes from "finding out the first things about people." Alice is an engaging creature, intelligent but ignorant, unconscious of the power of her beauty, eager for the knowledge which she expects experience to bring. She looked a little like St. Cecilia and glowed with an inner core of spiritual integrity which too few heroines of modern fiction have possessed, since so few modern authors set much store by it.

Alice learned about life from the guests in a near-by summer hotel, particularly from the young men. From one she learned about poetry and time and change, and from another about love, particularly how it could be a much simpler thing than she had feared. And from watching others she learned about passion and sin, death and tragedy.

Anne Goodwin Winslow has an uncanny way of suggesting character with a minimum of words, a few revealing scraps of conversation, a few significant thoughts and deeds. Although she is never obscure, she has a way of saying something so quietly that its implications are not immediately apparent, but only after one has paused a moment and let them sink into the mind. She frequently is witty, too, in a decorous fashion.

And most striking of all is the subtle skill with which she charges *The Springs* with a sort of still intensity as if all distracting sounds and trivial interruptions had been eliminated, leaving only the essence of her story, which is the illuminating experience of sharing with Alice her introduction to life. Since Mrs. Winslow is wiser and Alice nicer than most of us the experience is rewarding. It casts fresh light on familiar problems. It stimulates reflection and induces humility. *The Springs* is very good.

After two such lovely books it is not to be wondered at that Mrs. Winslow's fourth novel, her sixth book in eight years, was a disappointment. *It Was Like This* contains some shrewd truths and some shining phrases; but as a novel it is a frail and wispy performance. Its characters move through its twilight pages like impalpable ghosts, talkative ones. They plunge too quickly into contemplation of the great abstractions and do not seem to be speaking in their own voices, but in Mrs. Winslow's. They have little reality and little interest of their own.

But what matters about Mrs. Winslow's work is not that two of her books are inferior to the others, but that four of them are so good. It is good for the soul to know that they exist and better still to forget for a while the world that's too much with us and to spend a few rewarding hours in the company of a writer who still cherishes integrity of spirit and a quiet mind, who still values the graces and amenities of civilized living.

To turn from the feminine subtleties of Rumer Godden and Anne Goodwin Winslow to the vigorously masculine work of Dan Wickenden may, at first, seem too abrupt a change of critical pace. But I believe that Mr. Wickenden belongs in this chapter because, like the two women, he writes about shades of character and problems of personal relationships with generosity and tolerant wisdom, with an understanding of human behavior based on a sincere affection for people which is never vitiated by sentimentality. And I believe that Mr. Wickenden has not yet received the critical recognition which he deserves.

Dan Wickenden is one of the ablest of contemporary American novelists. Since 1937 he has written five superior novels, two of them works of substantial scope and unusual literary skill. A smooth and expert craftsman in fiction, he is a master of revealing dialogue. He knows how to let his characters characterize themselves in natural, individual and often humorous talk. His books are not notably funny, but they all glow with a delicious sense of humor which stops just short of open laughter. Mr. Wickenden has a quiet, sure sense of the drama that lies in the clash of personalities and of the inner conflicts which shape all human existence. His prose is simple, but suggestive and sometimes beautiful.

These are hardly common literary virtues. But, perhaps because Mr. Wickenden writes of decent and representative citizens and does not concern himself with either violence or degeneracy, perhaps because he is neither shocking nor obscure, he has not yet been considered as seriously as numerous other writers of nowhere near his stature.

Mr. Wickenden's first four novels were studies of American family life done with affectionate warmth and impressive exactness of observation. All five of his books are accurate accounts and subtle interpretations of life as it is lived by many Americans today. His books are not only entertaining and moving fiction; they are good social reporting.

In his first novel, *The Running of the Deer,* and in his second, *Walk Like a Mortal,* Mr. Wickenden wrote engagingly and perceptively about adolescents in upper middle-class families on Long Island, his own native heath. In his fourth, *Tobias Brandywine,* he wrote with equal charm and more humor, but with considerably less narrative and emotional power, about a family of adults. But it was with his third and fifth novels that Mr. Wickenden really showed what he could do.

The Wayfarers is a long novel about Norris Bryant and his family. It is laid in the Michigan city of Broadfield and takes place during the war years. The Bryants are pathetic and frustrated and unhappy, and exceedingly human and interesting. Mr. Wickenden has said some true and important things about them. There, in Norris Bryant, but for the grace of God, go many of us. His adoration of his wife, his crack-up after her death, his failure to understand or help his children are experiences that cut near the bone.

Norris had not asked much nor expected much as long as he could worship his Laura. When she died he tried to anesthetize his pain in drink. Years later he realized with a shock what he had done, how he had neglected and lost his children. Trying to make up for his sins as a father, Norris found his task incredibly difficult. Everything seemed to go wrong so that at times Norris and the children thought that there must be a blight on the family.

The stresses and conflicts of family relationships can be hard indeed to bear. To love but not to be able to guide or help is no small cross, although a common one. But in spite of folly and stupidity and hate and malice most people in the world and in Broadfield have more good in them than bad. Life with love in it for others is never without joy and beauty and great rewards. Mr. Wickenden demonstrates this old and never trite truth in the growth and development of his characters.

In the process he tells an engrossing and moving story. His mastery of his material, the adroit ease with which he balances inner conflicts with exterior action, his simple, fluent and witty dialogue are all exceedingly impressive. The many characters of *The Wayfarers* are all well rendered, the shoddy, cheap and malicious as well as the troubled, bewildered, decent and aspiring.

The Wayfarers is a novel of dramatic force and emotional power, of depth and solidity. Its roots are deep in Michigan, but its significance is universal. And in spite of its preoccupation with painful problems, it is filled with sunshine and warmth and honest liking for people. One feels after finishing it that one's knowledge of one's fellow human beings has been perceptibly increased and that one's sympathies have been widened. And that's a lot for a novel to do, one of the finest things a novel can do.

Dan Wickenden's fifth novel, *The Dry Season,* is a long and engrossing story about five major characters and a dozen minor ones. It is also a wonderfully evocative picture of Guatemala, where its scene is laid. And because of the nature of its principals and the circumstances of their life in Guatemala it is a delicate and yet striking dramatization of the neurosis of our time. Mr. Wickenden's five protagonists suffer from the usual fear and doubt and sense of guilt which beset sensitive people in the atomic age, the age, as Mr. Wickenden calls it, of "self-pity and water-tight excuses." But they are not the customary whining intellectuals of much modern fiction. They are troubled, but attractive, likable, amusing people.

In Guatemala they all hoped to escape from something and to find something. Their flight and their search were simplified for them by Guatemala itself, by the spectacular beauty of its scenery, the ready-made object lessons supplied by other members of the foreign colony and by the Indians. Mr. Wickenden does not indulge in foolish raptures about the superiority of the

[217]

Indians' primitive culture, as so many writers do. He is content to let the Indians' quietness, courtesy and pride, their delight in life itself, be an influence rather than an inspiration.

Long before the end of *The Dry Season* one becomes extremely fond of several of Mr. Wickenden's characters—for he possesses the old-fashioned ability to inspire affectionate concern without slipping into the quicksands of sentimentality. *The Dry Season* is a gentle, serene, placid and thoughtful novel about attractive people involved in complicated and significant emotional and intellectual problems. It is quite touching in its restrained way and filled with true insight.

This last quality springs chiefly from Mr. Wickenden's unusual sense of life, of the mixture of pain and joy, of weakness and courage, of sorrow and happiness, which makes living itself such a paradoxical, surprising, fascinating business. And this is exactly the quality which distinguishes the work of Rumer Godden and Anne Goodwin Winslow.

XIV

GOD SAVE THE IRISH

The Irishman at his best "is like some mad king of legend, in a world of tamed, groomed citizens; at his worst he suggests some rather malevolent gnome from the roots of the hills."
—*Arland Ussher in* The Face and Mind of Ireland

That the best English is written by Irish authors is a highly partisan generalization that is not true now and never was. But that many Irish authors write English wonderfully well is incontestable. Has any nation of comparable size ever produced such a long list of distinguished writers, from Jonathan Swift to Anne Crone? There must be something in the Irish climate, or in the whisky, or in the character of a passionately romantic and rebellious people, that is favorable to literature. Ferocious satire or moon-struck sentimentality flourish equally well on Irish soil, along with every intermediate stage between those extremes. Bad Irish writing can be as bad as any; but good Irish writing often seems to be marked by three peculiarly Irish virtues: humor, intuitive understanding of the sorrow and suffering of life, and an uncommonly delicate ear for the music of words.

These are considerable virtues and they do much to account for the special flavor of Irish writing. But there is another reason which may be as important in explaining the powerful appeal of modern Irish literature to those who care for it. And it is that in Ireland alone mature and thoughtful men are writing as if the world were little different from what it was fifty or one hundred years ago, as if personal problems were the only problems, as if they had never heard prophecies of doom or seen portents in the sky.

Ours is an age of fear and of the cruelty bred by fear. Ours is a time of agonizing doubt, or of false certainty fed on credulity and fanaticism. American and English writers reflect all this in their work, as they needs must and should, and their books in consequence add fuel to a roaring fire. But in Ireland the old men talk and the children play and the writers record their talk and their play with loving care. And they are neither angry nor afraid.

In the Pope's green isle they still sing "The Minstrel Boy" and "The Low-backed Car"; they still dance furious folk dances which are exacting tests of athletic skill and muscular co-ordination; they still twist the English language into lush, poetic lilting music; and they still walk hand in hand with sadness, futility and a resigned desperation indistinguishable from the spiritual climate of Chekhov and Turgenev. These practices continue as if the worst problems facing the modern world were the partition of Ireland, as if the most heroic struggle in which modern men have fought was the Easter Rebellion of 1916—and this last in spite of the fact that many thousands of Ireland's young men fought manfully in both World Wars.

The two contrasting strands of melancholy and humor are still twined tightly together in most Irish fiction. The melancholy is inclined to be ironic and is often bitter, for Irish writers, who care passionately about the abstractions of nationalism and religion, have few illusions about the sinful nature of men and women and the prevalence of poverty, ignorance and bigotry. The humor no longer is a matter of professional Irishness and Celtic charm. It springs from a relish in the absurdities and persistent follies of people and may be either affectionate or sardonic.

Irish fiction, it seems to me, is more likely to be constructed artfully and written precisely and poetically than English and American, particularly than American. In this country we have long overvalued vigor and freewheeling, undisciplined talent at the expense of literary form. To some Americans Irish fiction even seems naïve, since it is not brassily sophisticated and it is invincibly chaste. But it is a glib and superficial verdict which can dismiss writers like Frank O'Connor and Seán O'Faoláin as naïve. They are not.

But some of the characters they write about are naïve. And nearly all Irish fiction is written about people who accept the teachings of the Roman Catholic Church without question; most of it is written by authors who do likewise. It makes quite a difference in the general climate. Religion is not often discussed in Irish fiction. It is the way religion affects daily living that is a constant theme: the influence of the clergy, the young people who plan to become nuns and priests, attendance at Masses and confession.

The one subject which delights Irish writers the most is the never-failing marvel of the Irish variety of human character: the astonishing, exasperating, pigheaded, patient, heroic and endearing ways of men, women and children. Idiosyncrasies belligerently clung to, eccentricities shouted from the housetops, malicious gossip and saintly self-sacrifice, as long as they are the natural expression of real human beings Irish writers seize upon

[221]

them. Character with the bark on—that's what you can expect to find in Ireland as reported by her writers.

Probably the most versatile contemporary Irish man of letters is Seán O'Faoláin. Since 1932 he has written nearly twenty books—novels, collections of short stories, biographies, books of travel and literary criticism. He has also produced a considerable body of literary journalism. All his work has been distinguished by a deep understanding of character, by poetic feeling and by his mastery of various styles, from a pure and limpid simplicity of expression to a showy and glittering formality. Like most of his literary generation he took part in the "troubles." He says that he was educated "mainly by good conversation." But he has been a prodigious reader in world literature, particularly in French and Russian.

In the last ten years Mr. O'Faoláin has written a biography of the sixteenth-century Irish chieftain who fought the expeditionary forces of Queen Elizabeth, *The Great O'Neill;* an analysis of the national character of his countrymen, *The Irish: A Character Study;* a book about travel in Italy, *A Summer in Italy;* a book of criticism, *The Short Story;* and a collection of fifteen short stories, *The Man Who Invented Sin.*

These last are definitely superior tales, and taken together they are moderately impressive. But somehow they seem like small potatoes (Irish ones) compared to Mr. O'Faoláin's first and best novel, *A Nest of Simple Folk.* They lack the biting humor and robust vitality of the short stories of Frank O'Connor. Nevertheless, several of them are gravely beautiful and several are pleasantly humorous.

These gentle, thoughtful stories are never about dramatic crises, peaks of emotion or violent circumstances. Most of them are accounts of quiet little episodes written in a minor key, with affection, with melancholy and with deft and subtle implications about the meaning of typical situations in Irish life. The three themes which recur most often are memories of childhood, attitudes toward death, and studies of the clergy. Several of the humorous stories in *The Man Who Invented Sin* are not really funny, being diverting rather than comical, just perceptibly satiric rather than openly mocking. Their humor, as is the rule in Irish fiction, is mixed with pity and with sadness.

Like Mr. O'Faoláin, Frank O'Connor disparages his education. A scholarly librarian, he is a linguist, an authority on eighteenth-century music, the author of a book on Turgenev written in Gaelic, and of eighteen volumes of novels, verse, biographies and short stories. He has written more short stories than anything else and it is on them that his great reputation largely rests. The three collections of these which have been published in this country are *Crab Apple Jelly, The Common Chord* and *Traveller's Samples*.

A Frank O'Connor short story is not one of those slight and ambiguous suggestions of mood or character so beloved by many of our better writers today. Neither is it an old-fashioned affair, all plot, surprise and suspense. Midway between these extremes Mr. O'Connor takes his stand and draws little vignettes of life in which, if nothing much happens, a great deal is revealed. There is always meaning and point and form to his tales. They are always rich with human feeling and frequently they are wryly humorous. But they are less melancholy and less beautifully written than most Irish stories. Mr. O'Connor likes to write about human nature at its depressing worst; but his stories are not depressing. He enjoys life too much for that. He writes about people who are stupid, shallow and selfish, and obviously likes them just the same. His irony is practically cheery.

In My Opinion

Frank O'Connor writes with equal skill and understanding about old age and childhood, about saints and sinners. He can be tragic or grim or sardonic when he cares to; or sympathetic and pitying. But whatever his attitude, it is expressed with great restraint, suggested but never underlined. And all his stories are written with a precise exactness of phrase and an economy of words that are admirable. I have no doubt that he is one of the finest living masters of the short story.

The Irish talent for the short story is not confined to such distinguished and famous writers as Mr. O'Faoláin and Mr. O'Connor. Michael McLaverty, better known for his novels, has written fine short stories, and Bryan MacMahon, an extremely gifted newcomer, made his first debut as a writer of fiction with a short-story collection called *The Lion Tamer*.

Before that young Mr. MacMahon had kept a bookshop and written radio scripts, plays and poems. And he had won a name for himself as the author of a series of popular ballads in the traditional manner which have been sung at fairs and races by many a man who could not have said who Bryan MacMahon is.

Oh, Puck may be famous and Galway be grand,
And the praise of Tramore echo down through the land,
But I'll sing you a ballad and beauty extol,
As I found it long 'go in the town of Listowel.

Mr. MacMahon is a schoolteacher in Listowel, County Kerry, today and is at work on a novel which may have been published by the time these words see print.

The Lion Tamer is a collection of twenty-two short stories so good that they seem to me proof that Mr. MacMahon has joined the select company of Irish masters of the short story. He has a quiet wit and a frankly literary, poetic style which are peculiarly his own. Indeed, his style requires considerable mental adjustment on the part of a reader unaccustomed to prose so lovingly fashioned or to imagery so fanciful.

The stories in *The Lion Tamer* are less melancholy than is often the case in Irish fiction; and they are less comic. It is the middle of the road that Mr. MacMahon takes, recording significant moments, seemingly trivial but meaningful incidents, implying more than he actually says. He dwells lovingly on atmosphere, both the physical one of light and shade, wind and cloud, and the emotional one surrounding his characters. He writes always of simple people, farmers and laborers, nuns and children, portraying them in their impish malice and childish egoism, and also in their grief and frustration.

Another Irish schoolteacher with a wonderful way with a short story is Michael McLaverty, an Ulsterman who has written five superior novels and one excellent volume of short stories, *The Game Cock and Other Stories.*

In these twelve tales Mr. McLaverty always maintains the quiet mood of one thoughtfully recalling the past without idealizing it or indulging in nostalgic sentiment. His use of exact observation is as authoritative as that of the most heavy-handed realist. But Mr. McLaverty is selective. When he describes the dreary life of a Belfast street he achieves his effects with a few significant details and forgoes the pleasure of useless cataloguing. When he describes the routine of life on a lonely seaside farm he conveys both its unceasing labor and seasonal fluctuations without describing every forkful of manure in the manner of many "epics of the soil."

There are no neatly dramatic plots in these stories of the

wonder of childhood, the stale misery of age and the sour smell of poverty. But out of each small fragment of experience to which he turns Mr. McLaverty distills a satisfying emotion, a feeling of being allowed to share in his complete understanding of his universally human characters.

It is this sense of artistically rewarding satisfaction which is the chief pleasure to be found in *The Game Cock and Other Stories*. Gentle, restrained, told in a beautiful but austerely simple prose, all these stories are too cool and quiet to please undiscriminating tastes. They are not funny, angry, exciting, brutal or clever. They are only true and touching and exceedingly well done.

Many of them are about children. Without the precious attitudinizing which so often serves for a child's point of view in fiction some of them reveal more about the adults in the child's world than about the child himself. In other stories about lonely old age, about the selfish cruelty of youth and about the bitter frustration of poverty and pride and the conflicting demands of love and duty, Mr. McLaverty is equally expert. It would be possible, and perfectly reasonable, to prefer more bite, color and drama than Mr. McLaverty provides. But it would be impossible to deny that Mr. McLaverty knows just the note he wishes to strike and strikes it unfailingly.

Michael McLaverty is not always so impressive as a novelist as he is as a writer of short stories. His *The Three Brothers,* for instance, is a sound study in character, intelligently, neatly developed, written in admirable prose. Meanness, spite, shiftlessness and false pride are all demonstrated without anger as the deplorable failings they are. It is adroit and interesting; but it lacks the special flavor and lingering vibrations of Mr. McLaverty's short stories.

[226]

But in his latest novel, *Truth in the Night,* he achieves a memorable full-length characterization of an utterly obnoxious woman which is a triumph of objective understanding and cool pity. With all his customary technical skill and Irish artistry with words, Mr. McLaverty tells an intensely dramatic story, captures all the atmosphere of a small island off the Irish coast and lays bare the malignant soul of a bitterly unhappy woman. *Truth in the Night* is a profoundly moral novel written to dramatize its author's firm convictions about character and conduct. The truth about herself and selfishness which Mr. McLaverty's heroine learned in the night is one of the most important truths known to men. Mr. McLaverty makes it plain without spoiling his story by crude didacticism. *Truth in the Night* is too grim and harsh to achieve great popularity; but it is good.

There are so many Irish novelists now at work that if I tried to discuss them all this chapter would be stretched to an intolerable length. If my book is to be kept down to a manageable size only four more Irish writers will have to represent the rest. The first is Maurice Walsh, a writer who has not received the recognition he merits because his books are light and entertaining romances, superb ones, entirely outside the modern literary current.

Maurice Walsh, who says that his father knew all about horses and whisky, knows plenty about the same subjects; as why shouldn't he, being an Irishman, a sportsman and a writer? Since 1922 Mr. Walsh has averaged a novel every two years, a grand parade of highhearted adventure stories and engaging romances. His modern tales are delightful, and without any significance or serious literary intention whatever. His two historical novels, *The Dark Rose* and *Sons of the Swordmaker,* are grand, worthy to stand beside Stevenson and Dumas on your bookshelves.

For too long now romance has been the object of literary sneers. There have been plenty of love and an excessive pother over sex in modern fiction; but few indeed have been the good novels which have admitted that love can be a happy thing, that it can be felt by beautiful women and brave men—in other words, that it can be romantic. Usually the good writers have scorned romance, and the mediocre, sentimental, formula-ridden hacks have claimed it for their own and given it a bad name.

Novels without literary pretensions may be products of nice skill and artistically completely successful. A deftly written romance which triumphantly fulfills its modest purpose to distract and entertain surely has a better claim on our respectful attention than a dull and inept novel which aims at lofty heights of literature and falls miserably short of them. There aren't many books of this nature, I admit; or, if there are, I have missed them. But the novels of the late John Buchan fit the bill exactly and so do those of Mr. Walsh.

The last three Walsh novels are *The Spanish Lady, The Damsel Debonaire* and *Trouble in the Glen.* The first and last of these are laid in the highlands of Scotland, the second in Ireland. There is no need to describe these tales in detail. It should be enough to say that Mr. Walsh is gallant and romantic and that he likes to write about love and the joy of honorable combat in a good cause. He has an old-fashioned sense of humor which is refreshing. It is both so gay and so dignified! The wisecrack is unknown to Mr. Walsh's characters; cynicism is beneath them.

The dialogue in his books is something very special: rhythmic, flavorsome, witty, formal, almost stately. Whether people ever

[228]

really talk like this is immaterial and irrelevant. It is fun to hear them do so in his pages. What it comes down to is that Maurice Walsh has style, not only in the literary sense, but also an individual style of character and personality like that of a handsome woman, a thoroughbred race horse, or a clipper ship.

He reacts with fervor to beauty in women and gallantry in men, to moors and mountains, to Celtic peoples with old customs and old loyalties—Scots, Irish and Basques—to hunting, fishing, fencing and the Roman Catholic Church. And these are fine and gracious things to stir the heart of an Irish writer and they are fine ingredients to stir into romantic adventure stories. His books are a total anachronism as far as the troubled modern mind is concerned, and therefore all the better fun to read. They are even anachronistic compared with those of his compatriots who do not share Mr. Walsh's delight in romantic storytelling.

To turn from Maurice Walsh to Francis MacManus is to leave a gay and sunlit world for an unhappy and somber one. Mr. MacManus' only important book to be published in this country is *The Fire in the Dust,* an expert and quietly moving novel written with pungent power and disciplined restraint. He uses words with precise skill, creating effects without straining for them. And he writes with pity and objective understanding about matters which might well lure him into bitter fury.

The Fire in the Dust is a terrible picture of the twisted puritanism of modern Ireland. Everyone in the small town of Kilkenny twenty-five years ago seemed to be cursed with a ferocious prudery not far from prurience. The schoolboys alternated between shamefaced propriety and foul obscenities. Brother Brutt, the schoolmaster, was hysterically determined to

[229]

find evil and sin where there was none. And Miss Dreelin, the old maid who kept the shop where rosaries, statues and holy pictures were sold, in her private crusade for holiness spread vicious scandal all over the town.

All of Mr. MacManus' characters are well portrayed, always in scenes of revealing action and dialogue. The first-person narrator, remembering what happened in his youth, is a subtler storyteller than he realizes. He tells what he saw and felt at the time and doesn't try to analyze character with greater understanding than he possessed as a boy. But he supplies the evidence on which the reader can go on to extensive ruminations of his own about the cussedness of human nature. And many of these are sure to be provoked by Miss Dreelin.

Although Miss Dreelin is one of the most dreadful human beings I have encountered in many years of close association with horrible people in fiction, she is neither a caricature nor a villainess. She is malicious, sanctimonious, hypocritical, mean and evil-minded. The scenes in which she holds the center of the stage are so painfully real and unpleasant that they leave a queasy feeling in the stomach. One wants to forget that Miss Dreelin is a pitiful psychopath and hate her as if she were Simon Legree. But Mr. MacManus never allows you to do any such thing. He insists that you should pity and understand as well as despise. And he doesn't moralize about it. He just shows that the gruesome Miss Dreelin is an unhappy human being driven by her private furies well along the road to madness.

Francis MacManus is severe in his implied criticisms of prudery, gossip and bigotry, but he is not bitter or even angry. This is the way some people are in a small Irish town, he seems to say. They are not deliberately cruel. Most of them are kind and decent folk. Their prejudices are reflections of the only life they have known, the exaggerated responses of an emotional people to their cultural environment.

Bigotry of another variety is the theme of Anne Crone's *Bridie Steen,* perhaps the best Irish novel of the last decade (Lord Dunsany thinks it a great one). It has a stature, a dignity and an integrity which most current fiction lacks. Its prose is gravely beautiful in a quaint, old-fashioned manner uniquely Miss Crone's own. It is richly alive, quietly humorous in a sardonic way, amazingly objective in its treatment of one of the most deplorable manifestations of human nature, the mutual prejudice and animosity of Catholics and Protestants.

Bridie Steen is a story of Ulster in the 1930s, but it might as well have been laid in the 1880s. The Irish are not a people noted for rapid changes. They cling to their accustomed ways and their ancestral prejudices with unholy fervor.

Bridie was a lovable, not very bright girl, naïve, loving, timid, sensitive and emotional. She was easily frightened and easily moved to tears. But she had a fine pride of her own. She was a Catholic. Her Aunt Rose Anne, a fanatical zealot, had impressed on her the nature and importance of the river of darkness which flowed between good Catholics and evil Protestants. But Bridie had to live with her grandmother, who "couldn't abide priests about the place," who considered Protestantism a holy cause and the Catholic Church an evil conspiracy. And then Bridie had to fall in love with a freethinking Protestant. The pressures she was subjected to were nearly more than she could bear. Bridie's tragedy is Miss Crone's protest against bigotry.

Anne Crone is still another of Ireland's talented schoolteachers. She is a born novelist, equally adept in portraying character or in rendering the rural Irish scene. She writes of

Bridie with tender pity, of the other members of her cast with objective understanding. Her sardonic gibes at stupidity and hypocrisy are balanced by touching tributes to kindness, loyalty and love. It is this judicious sense of balance, an impartial appreciation of both sides, which is the most striking quality of *Bridie Steen*. Catholic faith and Protestant zeal are treated with equal understanding and the hatred and bigotry of both are condemned with equal justice.

As second novels which follow unusually fine first novels so often are, Miss Crone's *This Pleasant Lea* was a disappointment, but not a complete one, for it has extremely attractive qualities. It is the history of Faith Storey, the daughter of a farming family which had come down in the world through mismanagement and debts, and of her successful struggle to preserve her spiritual integrity while beset by the folly and vacillating behavior of several persons near and dear to her whose characters are much weaker than her own. It is written with the sweet and formal gravity that marks Miss Crone's special approach to fiction; but it lacks the sardonic bite, the rich vitality and the dramatic power of *Bridie Steen*.

This Pleasant Lea is not without charm and not without flashes of tolerant wisdom and sharp insight. Miss Crone's knowledge of character is impressive. Her love for the beauties of rural Ireland is engaging. Her demonstration of the unreasonable folly of social snobbery and arbitrary class distinctions is sound. But most of her characters are dull and colorless, and Faith herself is passive and dull, too. Rarely in Irish fiction have so many limp and spineless people been assembled in one book.

Nevertheless, Miss Crone is young and the author of *Bridie*

Steen. Her future is bright, and the Irish ought to be proud of her.

Less concerned with social criticism than *The Fire in the Dust* and *Bridie Steen,* and even more beautifully written in its lyrically Irish way, is *Rain on the Wind* by Walter Macken, an actor, playwright and novelist. This is a rarely lovely book, a fine combination of narrative skill and tender affection for people. Doesn't it take an Irishman, anyway, to be tender in print without being sentimental? You can find laughter and drama in *Rain on the Wind,* and that is all to the good; but you can also find the true wisdom of the heart, and that is not to be come by every day in life or in literature.

Rain on the Wind is only the story of a poor Galway fisherman. It is simple, unpretentious and as clear as spring water. It is very good indeed.

Its hero is Mico Mór, who "never wanted anything but to be a fisherman and to be at peace and to have a quiet life." But Mico was cursed with a disfiguring birthmark, and "a blind cod could see that he hadn't a brain in his head." It was Mico's brother, Tommy, who was the clever one, and handsome, too.

Mico Mór is one of the most appealing characters in recent fiction. His lack of brains was a matter of the intellect alone. His basic intelligence, his ability to face life and to judge between practical or moral issues, was great. Mico's kindness, loyalty, affection for his friends and courage were all unusual. Everyone liked Mico, "the big eejit," and everyone knew that he would never be anything except a poor fisherman.

Rain on the Wind is written in a series of dramatic episodes which provide a rich and fascinating picture of life in Galway. Local ways of speech, habits of thought and traditional customs fall neatly and naturally into place. Mr. Macken hasn't just written an immensely entertaining story about a likable hero. He has delved deeply into one corner of Ireland and done much to deepen his readers' sympathies. Any sensitive reader of *Rain on the Wind* will never again be so hasty to judge unfavorably an outwardly stupid person. Maybe, if one only knew him better, as well as Mr. Macken makes Mico Mór known to us, he would turn out to be as fine a person.

The writers of Ireland are blessedly and wonderfully outside the main stream of modern thought. But they are thoughtful men and women and fine writers. Without them the world of fiction would be much the poorer. A wonderful people, the Irish, God save them!

XV

FOUR GREAT NOVELS

"For thou hast made him a little lower than the angels,
and hast crowned him with glory and honor."
—*Psalms, 8:5*

Up until this point in our discussion of some representative
modern novelists, the nature of their achievement and the ideas
which they champion, we have encountered a wide variety of
good, bad and indifferent books, but no great ones. Several of
the novelists, Conrad Richter, A. B. Guthrie, Jr., John P. Marquand, Joyce Cary, James Gould Cozzens, Rumer Godden,
Anne Goodwin Winslow and Dan Wickenden, are the object
of my enthusiastic admiration. I have derived intense pleasure
from their books and for years have done my best in print, on
the lecture platform and in private conversation to spread the
good news, to persuade others that the art of fiction is flourish-
ing still and that truly fine novels await their attention. But I
have not claimed that any of the books written by these excellent
novelists are "great."

A critic soon learns to treat that dangerous word with gingerly
caution. If he doesn't it will bite him. Because he is so accustomed to reading mediocre books he is exposed to the occupational hazard of overgenerosity to good ones. If in his first flush
of enthusiasm for a good book he calls it great he may be terribly

embarrassed in a few years, or even in a few months, to have his unfortunate choice of an adjective flung in his face. Books, like flowers, often wither with distressing speed. The beauties which we first found in them have an alarming way of disappearing altogether.

In addition to his personal experience of the danger of excessive enthusiasm a critic is always aware of the ghastly blunders which deface the history of criticism. Truly great books like *Moby Dick* or *Huckleberry Finn* have been ignored or denounced. And books that are only pretty good, mediocre books and downright bad books have been acclaimed as immortal. A conscientious critic, always an evangelist at heart, wants to give every book its due, or more than its due. But he doesn't want to make a fool of himself by discovering a new genius every publishing season. Nevertheless, I believe that there were four novels published in the last decade which have reasonable claims to greatness.

What quality must a novel have to justify the use of so big a word? Obviously that quality is something extra, something in addition to the ordinary attributes of superior fiction. Thus, any fine novel must be written with sound craftsmanship, must create interesting characters and involve them in a significant situation, must reflect the special personality and point of view of its author. A great novel must do all these things, too, and do them superlatively well. But the extra quality of greatness lies elsewhere.

If the four novels of recent years which seem great to me are a fair criterion, that extra quality can be imparted by either of two things. The first is a feeling of passionate participation in life, an ability to celebrate life itself as a tremendous experience filled with joy and wonder and excitement, and with sorrow

[236]

and suffering. Such a feeling springs from a vital concern for human beings, an intense awareness of them and affection for them. This attitude does not depend on any particular dogma, religious or philosophical; but it does depend on a certain largeness of mind and warmth of heart. Great novels are not born in petty minds.

The second factor which can add a quality of greatness to a good novel is more specific—belief in the essential dignity of man, in the capacity of some men to rise to peaks of wisdom, unselfishness, courage and heroism. A novel acquires an added dimension of greatness when its author believes that people can be great. A great novelist in this sense is one who regards the sorry record of human malice and stupidity without evasion, but who recognizes that the vast spectacle of mankind's misery and suffering is shot through with deeds of valor and sacrifice, illuminated by love.

Although the majority of men are afflicted with sadly human failings, the majority are decent (though bewildered), well-intentioned (though ignorant), idealistic (though often led astray). The great truth about mankind is that many men have had visions of nobility and that a few men have striven to attain it. The novelist who shares this vision of nobility sometimes renders his book great by making it a testament to his belief that men and women may rise above their basest instincts, that they may enlist in the armies of righteousness and do battle for the Lord.

Both these attributes of greatness seem to me present in the four recent novels which I believe great; but it is the vision of nobility that particularly enriches *The Wall* by John Hersey, *Cry, The Beloved Country* by Alan Paton, *The Golden Warrior* by Hope Muntz, and *The Root and the Flower* by L. H. Myers.

In My Opinion

In Chapter X tribute was paid to John Hersey's accomplishments as a war reporter and as the author of an excellent war novel, *A Bell for Adano*. *The Wall* is a war novel also; but it is much more than that. Like its predecessor, it was inspired by Mr. Hersey's experience as a war reporter and is an effort to preserve the essence of contemporary history in fictional terms. It does so with such tragic splendor that it is already one of the monuments of American fiction. That Mr. Hersey was able to write such a book, his second attempt at fiction, before he was thirty-five is one of the minor miracles of literature.

The Wall is a novel about the plight of the Jews of the Warsaw ghetto from November 1939 until May 1943, when only a few fugitives were left alive. Naturally, then, it is a chronicle of unimaginable disaster. But it is also a novel about the unconquerable spirit of man. There are horrors enough here to rend the heart and sicken the soul. But Mr. Hersey's emphasis is not on horror. It is on the human character in all its infinite diversity, its shame and degradation and its self-sacrifice and heroism. These are no wooden puppets about which he has written, but suffering people revealed with subtle skill and profound understanding as they change and react to one another and to the terror which surrounds them.

They are Jews, Eastern European Jews in all their traditional Jewishness, described by one of themselves, for Mr. Hersey's narrator, Noach Levinson, is a Jewish historian. *The Wall* is written entirely in the form of extracts from Levinson's notes. This method of narration adds enormously to the persuasive power and intimate authority of Mr. Hersey's story. Levinson's insatiable curiosity about his fellows and his belief that individual experiences are the essence of history make him an ideal commentator. This, one feels, is the higher truth of emotional reality. These fictional people will live and represent for years to come in the minds of legions of readers the real people who died in the Nazi abattoir.

But the eloquent illusion of Levinson's notes is obtained at a high cost. Hundreds and hundreds of short excerpts from imaginary journals make for slow going. Broken-off conversations, kaleidoscopic changes of scene, constant cross references to other entries impede the flow of Mr. Hersey's story. So it is all the more impressive that, in spite of its intricate, perhaps unnecessarily complicated, structure, *The Wall* by its very accumulation of dryly recorded detail is so powerful and moving.

Noach Levinson's notes describe the methodical extermination of some half a million people. But the mass horror is conveyed through the stories of a score of individuals, the men, women and children who constituted his unofficial family. Day by day he follows their stories, from the first days of uneasy hope, through the building of the wall around the ghetto, the scientifically increased persecutions, the "deportations" to the death factories and the final futile but magnificent defiance of the ghetto revolt.

One of the interesting and pathetically human aspects of the life of the doomed Jews in the Warsaw ghetto was their effort to live normally, even to be gay and interested in literary discussions and amateur theatricals. But as the sky darkened, as typhus and starvation and man hunts reduced their numbers, such efforts ceased. Rival organizations, Zionists, Socialists, Communists, various orthodoxies quarreled among themselves. And many individuals failed in the supreme test. They became collaborators, gangsters selling "protection" from the Gestapo, informers who thought that they could buy their own lives by the deaths of others.

In My Opinion

Noach Levinson's passionate identification of himself with all Jews did not blind his scholarly objectivity and turn him into a propagandist intent on casting all his people as noble martyrs. He was interested in the truth, and the truth included the scoundrels as well as the heroes. But many were heroic men and women who grew in love and fellowship and courage and in devotion to the teachings of their faith. The terrific adventures of those true heroes in the underground bunkers and sewers of the flaming Warsaw ghetto are part of the terrible epic of our time. Mr. Hersey has provided them with a magnificent memorial in *The Wall*.

The second modern novel which I dare call great is the finest I have ever read about the tragic plight of black-skinned people in a white man's world, *Cry, The Beloved Country* by Alan Paton. Without any of the blind rage which has led so many writers on similar themes into bitterness and dogmatism, without any of the customary oversimplification and exaggerated melodrama, Mr. Paton wrote a beautiful and profoundly moving story, a story steeped in sadness and grief but radiant with hope and compassion. He contrived for it a special prose of his own which is both richly poetic and intensely emotional. Anyone who admires creative fiction of a high order, anyone who cares to see how a thesis novel can be written without sacrificing artistic integrity, should not miss this notable book.

Alan Paton is a South African and his novel is about that beautiful and unhappy land. For many years he was the principal of the Diepkloof Reformatory, a Johannesburg institution for delinquent African boys. He has lectured and written on the South African race problem, but this is his first book. He brought to it a rare technical skill as well as the contagion of his love for Africa and her tormented people. He is a man who can see evil and greed and cruelty and tragedy and not sink into despair. He knows that simple human goodness can still be found in a weary world.

Cry, The Beloved Country is the story of the progress of a Christian in whose path many lions stood. The Reverend Stephen Kumalo was an *umfundisi,* or parson, of St. Mark's Church at Ndotsheni high in the hills of Natal. He was an elderly Zulu, quite unacquainted with the dangers which lay in wait for his people when they left their hungry, eroded country for the great city of Johannesburg on the Witwatersrand. There segregation, poverty, a fantastic housing shortage, temptation and vice destroyed hordes of young men who sought a living in the gold mines. Their tribal society with its ancient laws and customs and moral traditions had been destroyed by the white people. And it had not been replaced by anything else save police and courts and jails.

Kumalo went to Johannesburg to hunt for his sister and his son who had disappeared there. His search was a tragic one. He found his sister first, and she had become a prostitute. He found traces of his son. As he plodded from address to address, finding graver news at each, Kumalo realized that Absalom, his son, had descended into a bottomless pit. So when the good white man who crusaded for native rights was murdered, Kumalo was appalled but not surprised to learn that Absalom was the murderer.

Kumalo's pitiful martyrdom was not all bitterness. His friend, Msimangu, a fellow preacher, proved to be an almost saintly man. The young white man from the reformatory where Absalom had been confined was hot-tempered, but earnest and kind. The white man who was the father of the murdered man was the source of unexpected comfort. The meeting of the two grief-stricken fathers, the proud, silent, conventional Englishman and the humble Zulu, is the high point of *Cry, The Beloved Country*. Then all the complicated social and personal threads of Mr. Paton's story meet and are entwined together in a powerful and extraordinarily touching climax.

Cry, The Beloved Country consists of an amazingly deft fusion of realistic detail and symbolical synthesis of various points of view and emotional reactions. As a picture of the fear and suspicion and hatred which haunt all South Africans, black or white, it is brilliant. The whites, who are so few, are frightened by the blacks, who are so many. Education, public health, social advancements of all kinds are dreaded for their capacity to make the Negroes more insistent in their demands and more conscious of their power. A minority of the disinterested and farsighted whites—and Mr. Paton pays them full tribute—are fighting for social justice. But they themselves are doubtful if they can persuade the whites to love soon enough— before the blacks learn to hate too well.

In conveying his message Mr. Paton never once damages his story, never once mounts a soapbox to orate at the expense of his novel as a work of fiction. His men and women are intensely real and sympathetic persons. Their conversations and their inner monologues are warm with the breath of life, in spite of the cadenced, lyrical quality which distinguishes them. Perhaps people don't really think or talk with such simple nobility of expression; but they never spoke in Shakespearean blank verse either. It is the truth of the spirit that counts, not stenographic reporting.

Current fiction, while often competent, interesting and provocative, rarely discusses an important and controversial subject with both creative artistry and generosity of mind. Because

Cry, The Beloved Country is both so skillful and so generous it seems to me a great novel.

The greatness of Hope Muntz's *The Golden Warrior* is of a different sort. The nobility in Mr. Paton's novel springs from compassion and generosity of spirit; the nobility in Miss Muntz's from the courage and heroism of men and the tragic grandeur of its hero's imperfect character.

The Golden Warrior is a majestic, glittering, heroic book of epic stature and stark magnificence. Too austere and strange to catch the popular fancy quickly, it is destined, I believe, to be read with amazed admiration for many years to come. It is a tale about Harold of England and William of Normandy, at once a triumphant tour de force and a major work of fictional art.

It would be a gross injustice if *The Golden Warrior* should be mistaken for a mere historical novel, even for a superior one. It is far more than that. It is a saga of two authentic heroes and one of the great turning points of history, which re-creates the glory and the folly of the past with magical power. And it is a tragedy in the true sense of the word, the story of a genuinely great man, Harold, who was doomed to disaster because of flaws and failings in his own character. The sweeping action of this gorgeous chronicle would have made a fine theme for a Norse skald. The downfall of Harold would have been a perfect one for Shakespeare.

This is a chronicle of the sixteen years during which Harold rose from the status of a banished fugitive to be the mightiest man in England, vice king to Edward the Confessor and finally king himself, and then, soon afterward, a dishonored corpse on the battlefield of Hastings. It is told in a series of short scenes tense with drama, with extensive and wonderfully expert use of dialogue. Using only a reasonable number of archaic words for flavor and atmosphere, it still seems like a contemporary document without a trace of the modern writer's laborious research. And it is focused entirely on character and action with no space at all wasted on costume, weapons, architecture, etc.

Hope Muntz is a Canadian-born writer who has lived most of her life in England. She spent sixteen years, counting her exhaustive research, on this book. That her facts are correct is vouched for in a foreword by G. M. Trevelyan, one of England's most eminent historians. This book is fiction; but its authenticity is as great as careful scholarship can make it.

While *The Golden Warrior* is not a difficult book, it does require certain intellectual and emotional adjustments from its readers. The style is bare and forthright, artfully contrived to suggest lordly grandeur without being elaborate itself. The many characters, with their complex family trees, are not easy to sort out at first. The dominant note of high emprise and fateful decisions is sustained throughout and never varies. There is no change of pace, only the steady march of doom.

Harold is the tragic hero of *The Golden Warrior,* but William is not a conventional villain. Both men were great soldiers and great leaders of men. Harold could command his followers' love, William only their admiration. Both men were ambitious. Harold wanted to be King of England, although his claim rested more on his ability than his lineage; but he wanted to be a glorious, honorable king and he trusted others too far. William wanted to be King of England, too, and his claim rested on a trick and a forced oath. He wanted to rule for power's sake and trusted no one.

There is an almost Greek sense of remorseless fate working toward its inexorable ends in *The Golden Warrior.* Harold's father, the great Earl Godwin, had betrayed a sacred trust and his sin was a curse upon his children. Harold, who was so generous and gallant, so strong in his faith and so magnificent in battle, wanted too much to be a king. He made errors of political judgment. He lied for what he thought was a good end. He repudiated his "hand-fast wife," the mother of his six children, in order to make an advantageous political marriage. All these things were for the good of England; but they were for the good of Harold's ambition, too, and they troubled his sleep.

It is amazing to see how Miss Muntz without use of any of the subtleties of modern fictional techniques still manages to bring her characters to flaming life, not only the two protagonists, but a host of memorable minor characters, lords and barons, bishops and prelates, soldiers and thralls. Her dialogue is not encumbered with "thee" and "thou" and "zounds." It is crisp and direct and cuts to the bone, whether the matter discussed is one of military tactics or of ethics.

And when she comes to her great battle scenes, Harold's crowning victory over invading Norsemen at Stamford Bridge only nineteen days before Hastings, and to Hastings itself, she concludes her stirring tale in a blaze of glory. Never have ancient battles fought with swords and bills and axes been described more graphically or with more pure delight, the joy of the exulting warrior. How a woman could have written so entirely masculine a book as this passes understanding. *The Golden Warrior* is breath-taking.

Compared to the nobility of L. H. Myers' *The Root and the Flower* that of *The Golden Warrior* seems almost primitive; for Myers' book is a novel of contemplation instead of action, a philosophical novel instead of an historical one. Its nobility lies in the ethical doctrine which is its conclusion and in the idealism of the quest for that doctrine which runs through all of the long work.

The Root and the Flower is an omnibus volume which contains four separate novels. The first three, *The Near and the Far, Prince Jali* and *Rajah Amar,* were first published in the 1930s. The fourth, *The Pool of Vishnu,* was published in 1940. All four appeared together for the first time in 1947 after the death of their author.

This exhausting but enormously stimulating and beautiful book is that exceedingly rare delight, a novel of philosophical ideas in which the elements of creative fiction, subtly realized characters and a story of sustained interest, have not been omitted to make room for the philosophy. Leopold H. Myers was an accomplished novelist as well as a dedicated seeker of the highest ethical truth. The people of his imagination are a fascinating group quite brilliantly portrayed. Their story may move at a slow and stately pace, with constant pauses for long sessions of abstract dialogue, but it does keep moving against an exotic and dramatic background to a satisfactory conclusion. This conclusion is satisfying because it completes the philosophical argument which is the theme of *The Root and the Flower.*

Although it is a story of sixteenth-century India in the reign of the great Mogul Emperor Akbar, it is not an historical novel. The Indian scene is colorful, but unimportant. It is only a means of getting some perspective on man's place in the universe. The absolute rule of a tyrant who has his enemies trampled to death by elephants, the corruption and intrigue of a dissolute court, and the cruel contrast between the misery of the starving peasantry and the gracious, refined, cultivated and selfishly artificial life of the hereditary aristocracy are symbolical of nearly all civilizations. Myers' selection of Indians, the most religious-minded of all peoples, as his characters gave him an appropriate opportunity to explore the ideas which primarily concerned him.

He did so through the minds of a dozen major characters of whom four are the most important. And most important of these is the young Prince Jali, a precocious youth whose growing-up and approach to the beginnings of wisdom are the central structure of *The Root and the Flower,* a book which might quite accurately have been called *The Education of a Prince.* Jali learned at court about social rivalries, about politics, about sex and about society as a whole.

His uncle, Hari Khan, a brave, impetuous, highly intelligent border chieftain, taught him much, particularly about the code of an officer and a gentleman. His father, the Rajah Amar, taught him more. Amar was a Buddhist of the most classically austere variety, a wise, learned, saintly man. In elaborating Amar's opinions at great length Myers was careful to give a hearing to Amar's friends and enemies of other religious persuasions.

The result is a series of luminous dialogues about religion and philosophy, reality and illusion, value, purpose, the self and God. These are not simple; but they are so lucid and free of technical jargon and the customary ambiguities of philosophy that they are intellectually exciting. But, brilliant, wise and illuminating as many of these discussions are, Myers found them inadequate. They are too preoccupied with personal knowledge and personal salvation. There is a greater goal, he believed, than the achievement of individual religious certainty.

The greater goal must be social. The good life cannot be lived alone, but must be lived in the tumult of the world, for others. Prince Jali became convinced of this through the teachings of a Guru who evidently spoke for his creator. And the Guru believed that far more important than metaphysical problems and questions of faith and doctrine is ethical behavior on a humble, practical level.

As Jali exclaimed when he began to understand, "There is no danger in religion so long as it doesn't touch upon the question of money!" That is, no danger to the cruel and selfish who are indifferent to the suffering of others. The Guru's teachings did not consist of an elaborate scheme for the reform of society complete to the last tax and tariff statute. He did not advocate revolution. But if many people practiced his simple, generous, profoundly humble precepts the world would be more changed than by any number of revolutions. Perhaps the Guru's teachings were not so very different from those of Jesus.

In addition to its high seriousness, *The Root and the Flower* is distinguished by urbanity, wit and much beautiful writing. Its appeal is necessarily limited and it is not yet widely known. It is a noble and a great book.

XVI

THE ART AND MEANING OF FICTION

"The art of rendering life in fiction can never, in the last analysis, be anything, or need to be anything, but the disengaging of crucial moments from the welter of experience."—*Edith Wharton*

Several years ago I was asked to feel sorry for a young writer because he had to earn his living in a business office. Wasn't it a shame that he had to work from nine to five and so had no time to produce his masterpieces? Wasn't his lot as a sensitive intellectual in this age of clamorous crises nearly unbearable? With some dudgeon I expressed no sympathy whatever and indignantly denied that the mere desire to be a writer is a qualification for an endowed ivory tower in which to be one. I cited Hawthorne, whose duties in the customhouse and as a consul in the diplomatic service did not prevent him from writing books which have been well thought of; Trollope, who worked all his life as a civil servant in the British Post Office; Lamb, who did not feel abused because he spent his days perched on a high stool among the other clerks of the East India Company; and Cervantes, Bunyan and Marco Polo, who found imprisonment no barrier to authorship.

And as for the theory that intellectuals occupy an especially pitiable position today—that's ridiculous when we remember the many millions of persons whose lot is truly terrible, the victims of the totalitarian tyrannies. Did Sophocles, who fought the Persians, or Socrates, who fought the Spartans and saw the defeat of Athens in the Peloponnesian War, know a world un-plagued by war and dangerous ideologies? Or did Shakespeare, or Milton, or Goethe? The answer is that the true writer writes, whether he can live off his writings or not, whether the din of battle assails his ears and the shock of doubt and fear troubles his mind or not.

The modern world in which we are condemned to live through no choice of our own is a cold and drafty place. It offers no safe haven for the timorous. Most of the portentous questions with which it challenges us have no answers; or, at least, we have not found them yet. But the world has never been much different. Few men have ever found living in it easy. But to live in it with courage is a high adventure and to write about living in it with skill and understanding is a fine achievement.

There are no rules to guide a novelist in what he should write and very few that can tell him how to write it. He must write what he wants to write, about what he knows best and about what he feels most strongly. He must write as well as he can and record the truth as it is given him to see the truth. And if he wishes to attract any considerable number of readers to his book he must do three things.

The first is to persuade. A novelist, whether he is writing the most trivial of ephemeral entertainments or the most solemn and ambitious study of man's soul and his place in the universe, must make his characters seem believable. Readers will meet him halfway. They are willing to believe in the King of Elfland if the novelist makes him seem both kingly and an elf.

[250]

The second thing the novelist must do is to make his characters not only believable, but interesting people whose company seems worth keeping for several hours or several days. The easiest way to do this on a superficial level is to make some of his characters sympathetic and some not, and to involve them in conflict, the old heroes-and-villains formula. Then the reader can feel concern for the welfare of some of them because he has identified himself with them. And if the blacks and whites of heroism and villainy are washed out and replaced by the subtle shading of more complicated characters a more intelligent and critical reader will be attracted.

And the third thing the novelist must do is to remember that a work of fiction is a story which must be about something, whether flight and pursuit or an emotional or moral crisis deep within the subconscious mind. Narrative interest depends on a sufficiently dramatic central situation or conflict to make what happens next seem important. The reader must be made to care. His own emotions must be involved.

But if a novelist is a genius, and sometimes even if he is only greatly gifted, he can refuse to do any of these three things and still delight his readers by the orginality of his approach and the impact of his personality. This is the hard way and not many writers can take it, only a few in each generation, a Laurence Sterne in the eighteenth century, a Meredith or a Melville in the nineteenth, a Joyce or a Faulkner in the twentieth.

There are three varieties of successful novels (there is no point worrying about the thousand and one sloppy, gooey, foolish and miserable ways in which a novel can be a dismal failure) and the most successful usually are all three at once. The three are: an entertainment, a fictional work of art, an interpretation of life.

In My Opinion

Some readers and critics are inclined to look down their noses at fictional entertainment with a ridiculously pompous air of self-righteousness. Several years ago a talented American woman novelist and critic expressed in my hearing her conviction that in times of world crisis, general calamity and mass suffering there is no place for novels which seek merely to entertain.

A novel, she proclaimed, should at least grapple honestly with the great truths and emotional problems of human life and experience if it did not concern itself with urgent issues of war and peace. When I asked her if she never read just for amusement, just for relaxation or just to take her mind off her worries and compose herself for a good night's sleep, she said grimly, "No. Never. When I read I want something I can get my teeth into." And I had a mental picture of her worrying a $3.50 novel as a terrier a rat.

It is easy to understand how she felt. Any good reader feels the same way much of the time. But such a perfectionist standard of criticism upheld with such fervent moral earnestness is as blindly fanatical, as arrogant and as opposed to other people's pleasures as the fulminations of a seventeenth-century Puritan divine. If writers, readers and publishers paid any attention to it a great portion of the books which give the human race the most pleasure would be drowned at birth like kittens.

Surely there is a need and there will always be a welcome for adventure and spy stories, detective stories and even science fiction, a need for novels which retain the increasingly old-fashioned virtue of narrative pace, novels which are stories! Farcical novels, high and low comedies, fantasies and romances all have their place in a balanced literary diet. How much duller the world would be if Conan Doyle had never written about Sherlock Holmes, if P. G. Wodehouse had never invented Bertie Wooster, if Angela Thirkell had never taken over Barchester, if C. S. Forester had not chronicled the adventures of Horatio Hornblower! One of the differences between a free world and a totalitarian world is that in the free one the individual's tastes can be catered to and the amenities of life, such as light fiction and butter, can have a place, as well as solemn art and guns. Fiction which makes no claim to be anything except entertainment may not require much critical discussion; but it is one of the props of a civilized life.

The second thing a novel can be is a work of art. If it is to be one its author must have mastered the technical craft of writing fiction. This is not so easy as it looks, as many a hopeful writer has found out who thought that he had all the necessary tools when he owned a typewriter and some paper. A sound craftsman in fiction must be skillful in the use of words. He must know how to arrange them in the most effective patterns, be aware of their rhythms and connotations, humbly venerate that noble achievement: a good English sentence.

He must know how to create characters through dialogue, thought and action (not in unsupported statements). He must have the creative imagination to think his way into somebody else until, for the time being, while he is hunched over his manuscript, he is that somebody else, a mixture of himself and of what he knows and imagines about others. He must be a good observer and be able to remember colorful and factual details, rhythms of speech characteristic of different kinds of people, typical gestures and special habits. And he won't be able to do this unless he is always interested in people and always noticing them. He must know how to develop his story in dramatic terms so that his characters are revealed in their relationships to one another.

And, perhaps most important of all, he must look at the inchoate mass of human experience, so bare of tidy demarcations and neat denouements, and impose a form upon it, a pattern which will give it unity and clarify its meaning as he sees it. This form is obtained by skill in the art of selection, what to put in and what to leave out. What Edith Wharton thought should be chosen she expressed in her famous maxim for novelists: "The art of rendering life in fiction can never, in the last analysis, be anything, or need to be anything, but the disengaging of crucial moments from the welter of experience."

The more finished a craftsman the novelist is, the more concerned he is with this matter of selection, of including only the significant, of not burying his story beneath a mountain of documentation and useless cataloguing. After all, a novel is not primarily a sociological document. It is a story about people living in society. The best and most effective way of telling it, of disengaging Mrs. Wharton's "crucial moments," is by compression, suggestion and implication. The danger is that the novelist may become too fascinated by such refinements of technique and succumb to the false charms of ambiguity and obscurity. But this danger can be avoided if the novelist will remember that technique is only a means of telling his story, of conveying ideas and emotions. It must not be an end in itself.

The third thing a novel can be, an interpretation of life based on the author's experience, ideas, private vision and conditioned reflexes, has been referred to regularly throughout this book. It is the summation of a writer's literary personality, the essence of it as it is transferred into print. It is his way of looking at the world, his convictions about God, destiny, love, marriage, society, virtue, sin and the problem of finding a reliable baby-sitter at short notice. It is this vision, this total personality, which impresses readers more than anything else, which they remember long after particular fictional characters have faded from their minds, which is the most conspicuous difference among writers.

It is this vision which excites or amuses thoughtful and critical readers, which makes one writer seem infinitely more rewarding than another perhaps equally skillful, which makes the writer himself more important than his individual books. Most literary criticism is devoted to it; most casual literary conversation is about it. After all, there is little to say about light fictional entertainment beyond saying that it is entertaining. And there is little which readers uninterested or untrained in literary technique can say about a novel's artistic craftsmanship. But everyone who likes to read, who reacts strongly to books, recognizes the stimulating difference between Thomas Hardy's outlook on life and Jane Austen's, between John O'Hara's and Rumer Godden's.

Everything a novelist sets down in his book contributes to his readers' impression of his outlook and personality: his choice of words and subject matter, his attitude toward his characters (which can never be concealed no matter how arduously the novelist may strive for objectivity), his manipulation of events. Everything fits together like pieces in a puzzle until the novelist who has written a number of books has also written a self-portrait. His readers know how he thinks, what he believes and what he cares about. Often they know these things more intimately than they know them about their friends.

In this way fiction is a never-failing source of intellectual stimulation. From novelists, sometimes wise, sensitive and tolerant, sometimes bitter, prejudiced and angry, we learn how other people feel about life and character, how they felt in the past and how they feel today in circles and even in countries not our own. No one who reads the best fiction sympathetically and attentively can remain so parochially minded, so narrow in outlook, so uninformed about points of view diametrically opposed to his own, as he would be if he read only the sporting pages. Fiction is the great educator for millions of people from childhood to old age.

Just as we may profit in a general way from the personal vision of authors, so we may also learn specifically from novels. They teach us about human nature as revealed in the minds and lives of fictional characters. All of us lead restricted lives, see the same face across the breakfast table, encounter the same group of people at our work and see the same circle of friends in our leisure. We have no way of knowing what it is like to be a South Sea trader, an Arkansas share-cropper, a New York City advertising account executive or a Welsh coal miner except through fiction, or, although the opportunity comes rarely, through a good play. By learning about such people in books we become better informed about the varieties of human experience and, unless we have minds of wood and hearts of stone, we should become wiser, more sympathetic, more tolerant through this vicarious participation in the lives of others.

The mystery of human personality and character may never be solved to the satisfaction of both priests and psychoanalysts. Information alone cannot do it. With increased information about environment, heredity, psychology and the sex habits of five thousand American males we lessen the circumference of the mystery by only a minute fraction, remove only some of the fuzziness from around its edges. One of the basic and most difficult things for anyone to understand is that someone else does not think the same way, does not even inhabit the same world.

Knowing better through experience, we expect others to be logical when we are not logical ourselves. Conscious of our own sins of commission and omission, we irrationally insist that our children and friends have no sins of their own. We may learn the folly of such conduct; but we never learn not to be a little disappointed by the bewildering confusion of a world in which every individual is, to a certain extent, a traveler from another country, a country where the natives worship strange gods and paint themselves blue.

But, even if we persist in being human and fallible, we can learn a more understanding kind of humanness through fiction. The importance of novels as interpretations of life has never been properly recognized. They demonstrate it best when the novelists succeed in creating memorable characters who are significant for their individual, personal efforts to meet eternal human problems.

I do not believe that the novelist can succeed in this respect unless he himself believes in the individual worth and dignity of men, in men's capacity of choice and their moral obligation to choose as well as they can, in the something within them that makes them worth writing about, that makes them worth saving from atomic extinction and from totalitarian terror.

APPENDIX

SOME NOTABLE HISTORICAL NOVELS

The following list is not comprehensive. It merely cites some examples of superior historical fiction published in the last decade which I remember with particular pleasure. They all are marked by the virtues discussed in Chapter IX: sound technical craftsmanship; accurate historical background artfully introduced as the natural world which their characters take for granted; interesting and believable characters; a plausible plot without excessive sensationalism or ridiculous melodramatics.

RED ORME. By Frans Bengtsson. Epic adventures in the days of the Vikings written partly in the manner and wholly in the spirit of the heroic, ignorant, childishly violent Norsemen.

THE WORLD IS NOT ENOUGH. By Zoe Oldenbourg. Love, war and revenge in twelfth-century France and Palestine.

THE CORNER THAT HELD THEM. By Sylvia Townsend Warner. Thirty years in an English convent in the fourteenth century. The story of a typical medieval institution and a collective impression of many characters associated with it.

FERDINAND AND ISABELLA. By Herman Kesten. Of a queen who mistook her lust for power for the desire to serve God: a novel of religion, politics and power with many grim implications for the present.

AT THE MOON'S INN. By Andrew Lytle. Hernando de Soto and the sixteenth-century Spanish paradox of fanatical religious zeal combined with insatiable avarice and monstrous cruelty.

[258]

Don Pedro and the Devil. By Edgar Maass. Francisco Pizarro and the same subject.

Web of Lucifer. By Maurice Samuel. Cesare Borgia and the political morality of Renaissance Italy, also with many modern parallels.

The Dwarf. By Par Lagerkvist. The same subject as Mr. Samuel's novel, but as seen through the mind of a dwarf blind with hatred for mankind.

The Gay Galliard: *The Love Story of Mary Queen of Scots.* By Margaret Irwin.

Young Bess. By Margaret Irwin. The childhood of Queen Elizabeth.

Elizabeth, Captive Princess. By Margaret Irwin. The youth of Queen Elizabeth. Miss Irwin is also the author of several equally distinguished novels about the Puritan-Royalist Civil War. Probably she has written more fine historical novels than any contemporary novelist.

Good-bye, My Son. By Marjorie Coryn. Napoleon as seen through the eyes of his indomitable mother.

The Marriage of Josephine. By Marjorie Coryn. Napoleon and Josephine as seen through that illustrious wanton's own eyes. Both of these novels are brilliant examples of a flashy, impressionistic, stream-of-consciousness technique applied to historical fiction.

Beulah Land. By H. L. Davis. A picaresque and poetic novel about the American frontier from 1851 to 1861.